Create

Naturally

Other Schiffer Books on Related Subjects:
Organic Embroidery, Meredith Woolnough, ISBN 978-0-7643-5613-1
Painting the Elements: Air Water Earth Fire, Parramon,
ISBN 978-0-7643-5953-8
*Listening to Flowers: Positive Affirmations to Invoke the Healing Energy of 38
Bach Flower Essences*, Dina Saalisi, ISBN 978-0-7643-6379-5

Cover and interior designed by Ashley Millhouse

Type set in Azo Sans/Baskerville

ISBN: 978-0-7643-6434-1
Printed in China

Published by Schiffer Publishing, Ltd.
4880 Lower Valley Road
Atglen, PA 19310
schiffercraft.com; 610-593-1777

For our complete selection of fine books on this and related subjects,
please visit our website at www.schifferbooks.com. You may also write
for a free catalog.

Schiffer Publishing's titles are available at special discounts for bulk
purchases for sales promotions or premiums. Special editions, including
personalized covers, corporate imprints, and excerpts, can be created
in large quantities for special needs. For more information, contact
the publisher.

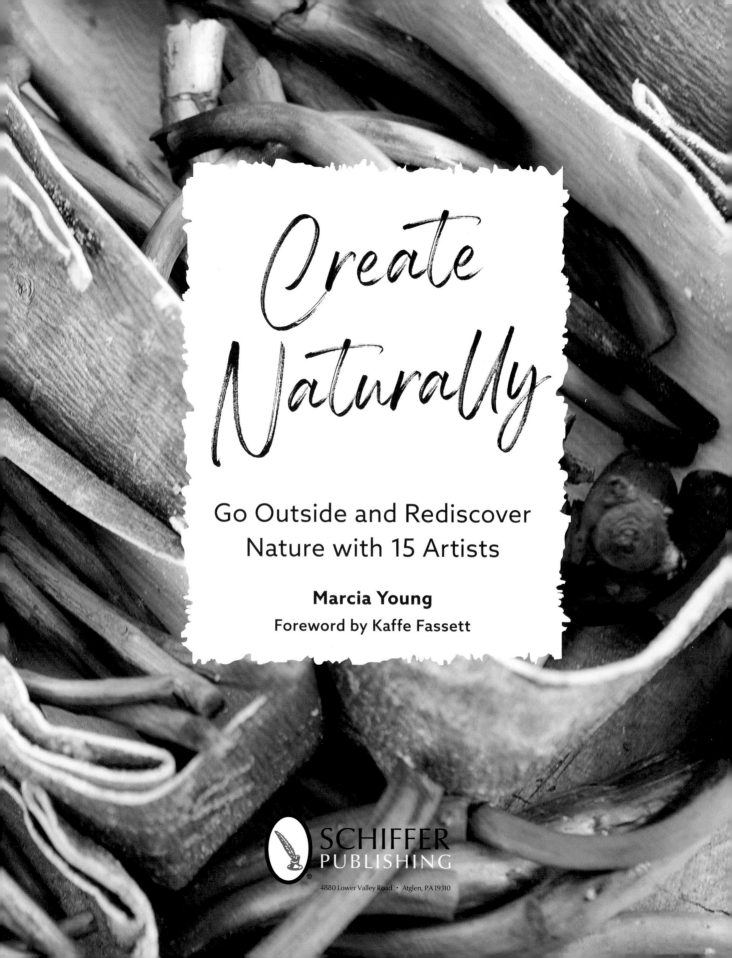

Create Naturally

Go Outside and Rediscover Nature with 15 Artists

Marcia Young

Foreword by Kaffe Fassett

SCHIFFER PUBLISHING

4880 Lower Valley Road • Atglen, PA 19310

Dedication

For my parents, Carl and Bev, with all my love.

For Jack, who lived fully and left too soon.

CONTENTS

When one tugs at a single thing in nature, he finds it attached to the rest of the world.

—*John Muir*

FOREWORD

Color has become my lifelong obsession and the element that unites all my talents. Making mosaics, knitting, stitching needlepoint, or creating patchwork and fabric prints are all ways of exploring and refining color for me. My work in textiles has helped me use color in my still-life painting in a more poignant way. This concentration on color seems to surprise some people, who state that form and storytelling are more significant in their textile pieces. If I encounter people intrigued but afraid to use color lavishly, I tell them to study children's art, which uses an unapologetically bright palette with great humor and directness.

How amazing that nature still knows how to renew itself in progressively delightful ways, and in doing so, helps renew our spirits as well.

"Cloisonne" in blue colorway, designed by Kaffe Fassett for FreeSpirit Fabric's Kaffe Fassett Collective

Photo: Debbi Patterson

I was born in the very urban city of San Francisco, so concrete and steep-hilled houses were my first perspectives. When I was eight years old, my parents moved to the remote community of Big Sur on the coast of California. At that impressionable age, I roamed the canyons, hills, and beaches, finding such treasures as acorns, pine cones, bird feathers, and animal skulls.

Shells and pebbles on the beach were exciting materials with which to create mosaiclike designs and then watch them be washed away with the tide. The colors of humble stones entered my consciousness there, so that the stone walls I encountered in Britain years later had me tuned in to the range of tones in those rocks. Small dried ferns that looked gilded to my child's eye had me imagining a whole minute world. I had to learn not to pick one of the most colorful items on our hills—leaves that turned brilliant shades of scarlet but would give you a deep-pink rash if picked—poison oak. Another vivid impression was the huge masses of succulents called ice plant. They not only turned every imaginable shade of green into maroon but grew sea anemone–like blooms of lavender pink with yellow centers. These grew in massive circles on the sandy soil of the coastal hillsides.

The mountains of California skewed green to gold, with grayish tones. The older I got, the more I appreciated the subtle world of weathered and faded surfaces I encountered: silvered wood, dried leaves and flowers, grasses, and gray-green sage. Combined, they created a close-toned world of great charm. When I got to Australia on one of my tours, I tapped into the organic world of Aboriginal art, a vocabulary of mainly natural earth tones in dots and lines. Though they use a limited palette, there is magic in their compositions.

My passion for color came mostly from other sources than the natural world. Theater was a world that awoke in me the strongest color highs. My mother would pull every string she could to get me to see whatever exotic production came to our nearest town. The fabulous Kabuki Theatre, with its colorful sets and dramatic costumes, was a feast for my imagination that continued to grow in my mind's eye long after seeing a performance. Balinese dancers and films such as *The Red Shoes* and *Henry the Fifth* were also huge in my child's eye.

As I grew old enough to travel and visit the world's decorative-arts museums, I learned that whatever color you wanted to employ in a design became more effective when organized into a pattern. As I gazed at embroidered costumes, painted furniture, and beaded objects, a strong sense of pattern brought the colors to life.

My travels to teach and lecture have taken me to every corner of the globe, so I was able to see firsthand how

Apple and Cabbage by Kaffe Fassett, 1997

African, Indian, and Mexican cultures arranged color. The Scandinavian countries have their vivid folk-art approach to decoration, and France, Italy, Spain, and Germany have definite styles and cultures that had me dancing with delight. Holland and Portugal stand out in my memories, with their wall murals on the streets and stairs.

What I learned from Japan, one of the countries most intensely playful with patterns, was a reverence for the natural world. A mushroom, a leaf, or a seashell is interpreted in myriad ways on kimonos, pottery, and painted fans. I came away from Japan with books, scraps of fabric, paper fans, and decorated objects, all containing great ideas for organizing colors in my textiles, pottery, and paintings.

Flowers came to the forefront of my design motifs when I entered the world of patchwork and was invited to do my own print ranges. Wanting big scale and lashings of color, florals were an obvious way to go. Cabbage roses, flamboyant peonies, and Easter lilies were wonderful vehicles for big splashes of color in my prints. I also became entranced by vegetables and fruit. Cabbages,

Swiss chard, and oranges featured in popular prints. Using the shadings and blushes of tones I'd observed in nature and the ethnic decorative renditions of flowers, I made my name in the patchwork world on upscale prints from the natural world. When Philip Jacobs joined the Kaffe Fassett Collective, his botanical prints and studies of shells became massively popular in our range. I do the colors for Philip's prints, so the whole fabric collection hangs together for quilters to add to their color palettes. Brandon Mably, the third member of the Kaffe Fassett Collective, plays with the patterns found on shells, snakeskin, and stripes inspired by nature also.

Needlepoint was a craft that allowed me to return to the themes of my paintings. For years, I'd done still lifes of patterned china and flowers on decorative cloths, inspired by the Asian delight in mixing patterns that I encountered in Persian and Indian miniatures. Taking a vase or bowl from my paintings and doing it as a cushion in the charming texture of wool stitched on canvas opened a new world of exploration for me. I was also featuring cabbages, cauliflowers, and every sort of bold floral I could find reference to in seed catalogs and classic Dutch, French, and Italian paintings. Early American folk art also provided great floral and vegetable references to stitch.

A vital aspect of all this creative activity is the light we see the world by. In California, there were, of course, some days that started and occasionally ended in fog or mist, but the average weather was bright and clear, which provided sharp light. When I got to England, I was delighted to find mostly soft, filtered light, allowing colors to glow in their more subtle glory. I arrived in a golden autumn where mists crept through the turning leaves and left dew on the end-of-season gardens.

I'm an early riser, so I loved wandering in the quiet mornings to see the delicate sunlight creep into gardens and landscapes. An English woman put it perfectly: "England has a pearly light." I fell in love with the variety of colors in the British autumn and winter. First the amazing colors of branches on garden shrubs and trees—some rhubarb pink to chestnut red, others lime green to high golden yellow. These made winter an unexpectedly colorful season. As spring dawned in England, I found more joy in the early crocuses and snowdrops that appeared on the still-frozen end-of-the-winter gardens. As I explored the cities, I was thrilled to encounter window boxes overflowing with colorful blooms, not only on domestic sills, but outside banks and other public buildings as well, giving such a boost to one's day. The love of gardening was such a strong element that it kept me happy in my new English home.

I am still in awe of how amazing a seemingly mono-chromatic copse of trees can be—those thousand and one shades of green and the varieties of leaf shapes. In my textile collections, I play with round lotus leaves, pointed coleus, geranium leaves, and all sorts of exotic palms and tropicals. The patterns within each leaf are a constant wonder and inspiration to me, making a tour of a botanical garden or a grand display like the Chelsea Flower Show a psychedelic experience.

Nature is an undeniable influence on my design work and good medicine for mental well-being. After this past year being locked in due to COVID-19, I found that my daily hour-long walks heightened my senses, so much so that local gardens and avenues of street trees totally lifted and inspired me. How amazing that nature still knows how to renew itself in progressively delightful ways, and in doing so, helps renew our spirits as well.

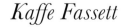

Kaffe Fassett

Introduction
LET'S START HERE

> Once we believe in ourselves, we can risk curiosity, wonder, spontaneous delight, or any experience that reveals the human spirit.
>
> e.e. cummings

This book has been patiently brewing in my subconscious for quite a while. Over the past fifteen years, I have spent most of my time writing, editing, or publishing stories about artists. I also have juried and curated many exhibitions and was the editor in chief of *Fiber Art Now* magazine for more than a decade. All of these projects have been driven by my unabashed curiosity about artists and what drives them. . I have found myself either formally interviewing or simply spending time casually with hundreds of artists. By now I have worked on myriad layouts, with an intense focus on finding the most effective way to showcase each artist's work and convey the process or message that they bring to the world through their work. These connections have happened in every kind of setting, from article interviews to chance meetings at exhibition openings to casual coffee klatch meet-ups, and countless other get-togethers that offered opportunities to connect. Throughout all this time and across countless situations, a disproportionate number of artists have shared that they are "inspired by nature."

Now, let me tell you something. If you and I were sitting across the table from one another right now, you would detect a very slight eye roll on my part. I know that many—maybe even a majority—of artists throw out a quippy "nature" reply when queried about what inspires their work. But for years, I have felt that reply was essentially offering me a commercial rather than the full documentary that I was looking for. It's an easy way out, a canned answer to what actually drives their creative process. I yearned to find something more. An original

retort *must* be behind the glib "I'm inspired by nature" reply that had been served up again and again, right? At least that is what I hoped. Certainly, if I followed this road with thoughtful attention, unique ideas would reveal themselves, allowing me to gain a greater understanding of the core connection that we all have to nature and why it is so much more than a pleasant inspiration. Integrating that knowledge will help all of us stop into more meaningful lives. Most of all, I hope to integrate the insights of this book into my life and invite you to do the same.

I selected each artist not only for the diversity of their work but also for their warmth and the sense of purpose that they derive from nature, each in their own way. Every one of them has connected with nature to build their art and to show how interactions with nature foster a state of flow that releases creativity, results in a keener sense of observation, and—most of all—enriches your life. At the end of every artist interview, you will find a "Go Outside" section where the artists share their personal, firsthand advice on how you can experience the awe and sense of wonder that they have fostered in their own lives.

So here we are. You and I, together, ready to approach the nature-creativity connection with fresh eyes, sans eye rolling. Cue upbeat, hopeful music here. We are about to learn how to integrate simple lessons from the natural world on how to increase creativity and foster more meaning in your life, whether you live and work in New York City, wake up every morning in a small town or suburb, or have a home on the edge of farmland, a mountain range, the coast, or the desert. It is there for all of us.

As I was originally digging into this topic, I came across the work of David Strayer, PhD, a cognitive and neuroscience researcher at the University of Utah. One of the areas he concentrates on is how attentional capacities can be restored by interacting with nature. He has officially coined this area attention restoration theory (yes, the acronym is ART). **But regardless of what research shows, we all have the deep, natural cognition to know that art and nature are restorative.** Dr. Strayer has simply brought measurable results to the conversation. His studies show that people have markedly increased capacity for creativity after spending time in nature. Even more, his decades' worth of research on the psychological and cognitive effects of the outdoors has proven that spending time outside enhances higher-order thinking and restores attention along with providing a boost in creativity.

I have selected these artists to guide all of us while we *naturally create* together. So, let's move ahead from here. Connect with them by starting at the first chapter and progressing through their personal stories, by wandering through each section to devour the images, or by skipping ahead to the first artist whose work sparks your imagination. Regardless of how you proceed, you can be inspired today, even if your first step is simply to resolve that your lunch break will be spent being present outdoors. Your heart will thank you and your creativity will blossom. With warmth and love,

Marcia Young

Bethan Burton
JOURNALING WITH NATURE

Love of nature is the spring from which
stewardship flows. In contrast, disconnection
from nature leads to apathy in the face of all
environmental problems. A useful way to define
love is sustained, compassionate attention.
Paying sincere attention to and developing a rich
curiosity about others helps us to be kind. This
attention takes work and improves with practice.
Whether with a child, partner, student, or
stranger, this practice changes who you are
and your understanding of your relationship.
You can do it with a loved one or with a
grasshopper or a blade of grass.

—*John Muir Laws*

Bethan Burton has an assignment from the universe, and she carries it out in earnest every single day.

Her mandate is to spread the word about how profound and magnificent this world is, and to celebrate that simple curiosity, which to her, holds the key to unlocking a life of wonder. She fulfills this mission through the art of nature journaling. The clarity of Bethan's life is borne from her extraordinary experiences.

This story begins with an adventure-seeking, dauntless young woman who set out to hike alone through New Zealand, parts of England, and several other European countries. She spent two years on and off the road, collecting experiences and connecting with friends along the way. Her intrepid character inspired her travels as well as her adventurous life.

After several years of sustaining her frenetic life, she began to lose her vigor. Energy drained from her body more every day. Her muscles hurt and she had trouble keeping up the pace of even an average day, let alone one of her more adventurous ones. Unbeknown to Bethan, she was developing a chronic illness.

Her condition worsened, and ultimately, she was relegated to her bed for almost two years. During those long days and in between medical appointments, the scale of her world drastically decreased from encompassing (literally) the entire world down to whatever she could experience from her bed or right near her home. "I thought, 'Who am I if I can't have the career I had hoped for myself?' I had to completely reframe my identity."

Not only was Bethan confined to her bed most of the time, it was even difficult to make her way to the mailbox every day. So she traded hiking the world for spending countless hours in her own backyard. In her words, "I remember it so well. It became a very important part of my day, for staying calm, centered, and connecting with something outside myself."

Because she had always loved art, she started writing about and drawing what she saw in her backyard. "I remember watching this huge eucalyptus tree. There was a family of crows living in it. Every day I would observe and sketch them, along with other nesting birds." These familiar rhythms and routines became her lifeline. She said, "You don't have to go far to find wonder. Even if you just part the grass in an urban yard, you can see so many things happening. We have a lot things going on in our lives, and, all the while, nature is continuing all its processes." During this time, she discovered that her observation skills became sharper.

After coping with several years of illness and researching her condition, Bethan learned that she was suffering from orthostatic intolerance, a condition of the autonomic nervous system. Her sister has the same condition, and together they were able to figure out how to make an upward trajectory and slowly return to a normal life. The entire experience resulted in an awakened sense of curiosity and awe about the natural world. Remarkably, during that time she also was able to earn a master's in environmental studies with a concentration in education and sustainability.

Bethan emerged from her illness as a different woman, one for whom experiencing nature and nature journaling became an integral part of her everyday life. "Nature and nature journaling drops me into the present moment. It helps me realize that everything is so simple when you are living in the world that we are so lucky to wake up in."

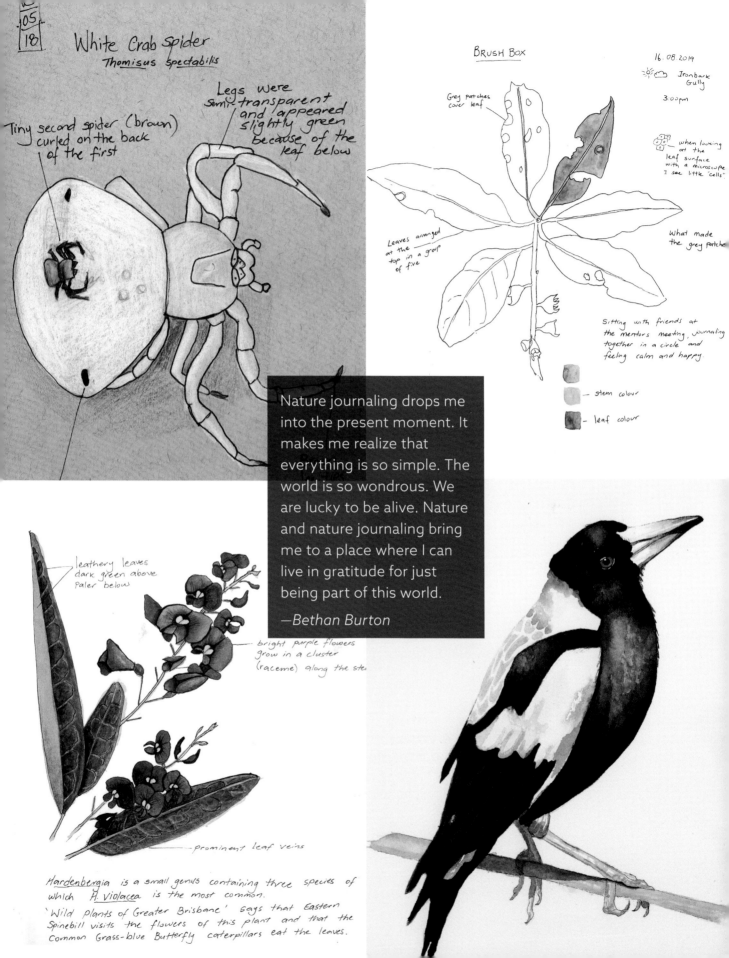

05
18

White Crab Spider
Thomisus spectabilis

Legs were semi transparent and appeared slightly green because of the leaf below

Tiny second spider (brown) curled on the back of the first

BRUSH BOX

16.08.2019

Ironbark Gully

3:00pm

Grey patches cover leaf

when looking at the leaf surface with a microscope I see little "cells"

Leaves arranged at the top in a group of five

What made the grey patches

Sitting with friends at the mentors meeting, journaling together in a circle and feeling calm and happy.

— stem colour

— leaf colour

Nature journaling drops me into the present moment. It makes me realize that everything is so simple. The world is so wondrous. We are lucky to be alive. Nature and nature journaling bring me to a place where I can live in gratitude for just being part of this world.

—Bethan Burton

---

leathery leaves dark green above paler below

bright purple flowers grow in a cluster (raceme) along the ste...

prominent leaf veins

Hardenbergia is a small genus containing three species of which H. violacea is the most common.
'Wild Plants of Greater Brisbane' says that Eastern Spinebill visits the flowers of this plant and that the Common Grass-blue Butterfly caterpillars eat the leaves.

Australasian figbird

Sphecotheres vieillot

Red mask around eye

Black head

olive green wings

♂

older fig

young fig

Actual size

Figs are different colours at different stages of maturity

black tail

I have been watching every day with my binoculars.

These birds are totally dominating the airwaves here at the moment. I know their call well now and it is certainly the most heard call each day.

holds berry/fig in its beak. Is this the reason for its slight hook?

I didn't know much about the figbird until recently. Brian's advice to focus on learning one bird at a time is helpful.

Yellow underside is it really yellow or does it just look that way in photographs? Look closer!

pink/red legs

The call is very varied, sometimes a chatter, sometimes distinctive two low notes and then a high note.

Beak has a slight hook which reminds me of butcher birds' beak.

eye mask colour

Fig leaves are thick and deep green. What species is this?

Just read that males in northern areas have a yellow front, but not here → IMPORTANT not to rely on photos

From photos I can see that the female has a very thin blue ring around her eye, but I haven't seen this yet in real life observations.

Tomorrow I will look out for her eye ring!

Female has white underside with brown wings.

underside is flecked with brown, downward stripes.

♀

Do females and males make the same call?

Are these birds here year-round or are they here just for the figs at the moment?

I often see the inside of the birds mouth because they are eating or singing.

How can I capture the call on paper? I wish I could translate the song into musical notes and write them down! Listening to them it's hard to capture just one sound. They chatter together almost constantly, back and forward.

22

24.2.19

The benefits of journaling were enormous for Bethan. These days, she is an enthusiastic advocate for nature journaling. "There are so many reasons for nature journaling. For example, it could be for scientific research reasons or for keeping track of the changes in your garden. My reason was for self-care. When you embrace the nature-journaling mindset of intentional curiosity and appreciation, then you can refine your awareness about even the most common things and realize that there is wonder all around you. John Muir Laws, an author and teacher of nature journaling, recommends finding ways to journal in everyday life, such as journaling from your refrigerator. He did it with an orange, and over time, he nature-journaled the aging of the orange. You can even find wonder in a moldy orange!"

Nature journaling blends Bethan's educational background with her passion for art and the environment. By 2015, she was tracking her daily activities on Instagram and was amazed by the warm, enthusiastic response she received. This encouraged her, and her community began to grow. "Building a following is not my thing. I am dedicated to connecting from the heart with genuine feeling and really building a community. Social media can be whatever you want it to be. It can be toxic and inauthentic or warm and genuine." Clearly, Bethan chose to utilize it to foster authentic relationships.

In the midst of these developments, a local community organization reached out to Bethan and invited her to present a nature-journaling workshop to a community group. That was her first foray into sharing the impact of her nature art journaling with others. She now regularly teaches a variety of workshops related to nature journaling, online and in person. With the COVID quarantine, she found that she could teach an impactful online course by using Google Earth. For one such class that focused on color, Bethan took participants on a virtual field trip, discussing the colors of a local eucalypt forest, and Uluru, a sacred place for Indigenous Australians. "Our class talked about how to mix that color and how the incredible rusty-red color changes at sunset and sunrise, so we did three stages as the sun was rising. That particular experience was part of the Wild Wonder Nature Journaling Conference, which was held virtually during the COVID pandemic."

Bethan also created a blog, where people from around the world have contributed personal stories about how their lives have been affected by nature journaling. That blog ultimately led to her podcast, *Journaling with Nature*. "It is magical for me; very uplifting and inspiring. I see my role in the podcast as connecting people with each other." Bethan found that every person has their own way of journaling and their own story for why they do it. She is driven by her desire to learn more and connect with them. The podcast helped her do that. "I was very unsure of myself at first, but it became natural. I realized that if I just do what I do naturally and ignore the flashing red light that says it is being recorded, I can authentically listen to someone's story and share it with the wider community. It has been amazing." Ever since she began to connect with others through the blog and her workshops, she has been developing nourishing, long-lasting friendships from around the world.

ALOE VERA

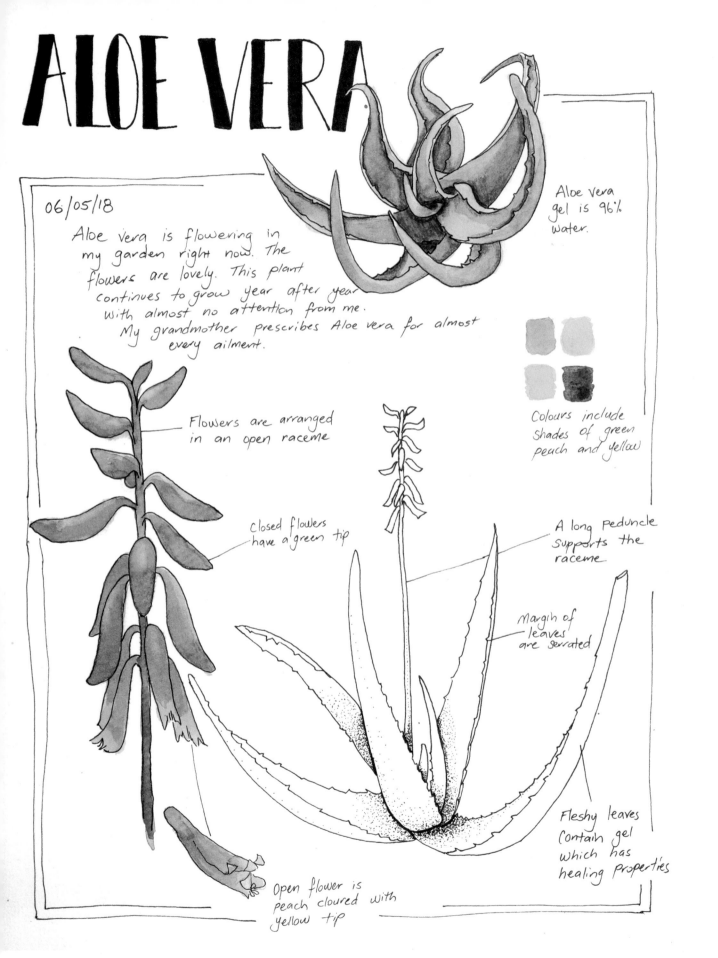

Aloe vera gel is 96% water.

06/05/18

Aloe vera is flowering in my garden right now. The flowers are lovely. This plant continues to grow year after year with almost no attention from me.
My grandmother prescribes Aloe vera for almost every ailment.

Colours include shades of green peach and yellow

Flowers are arranged in an open raceme

Closed flowers have a green tip

A long peduncle supports the raceme

Margin of leaves are serrated

Fleshy leaves contain gel which has healing properties

Open flower is peach cloured with yellow tip

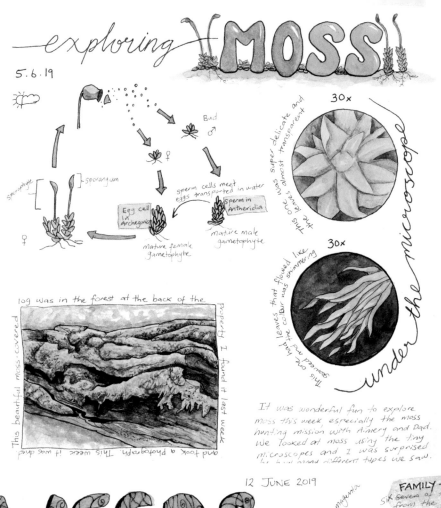

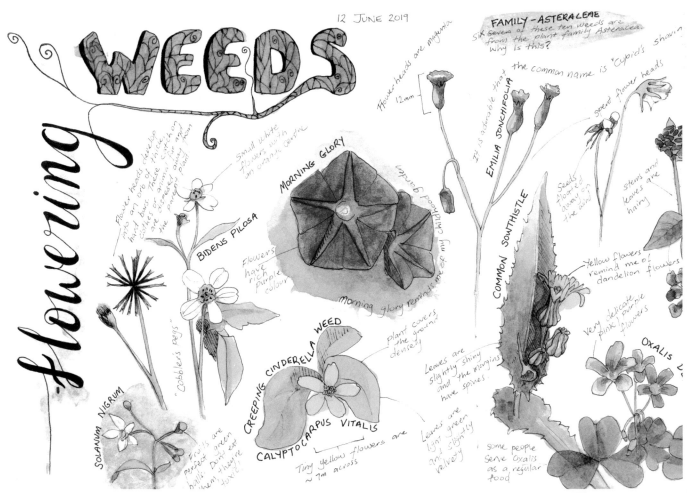

> When you ask people for their story and deeply and openly listen to them, everyone has something important to share. It is a heart-led and heart-opening experience.
>
> *—Bethan Burton*

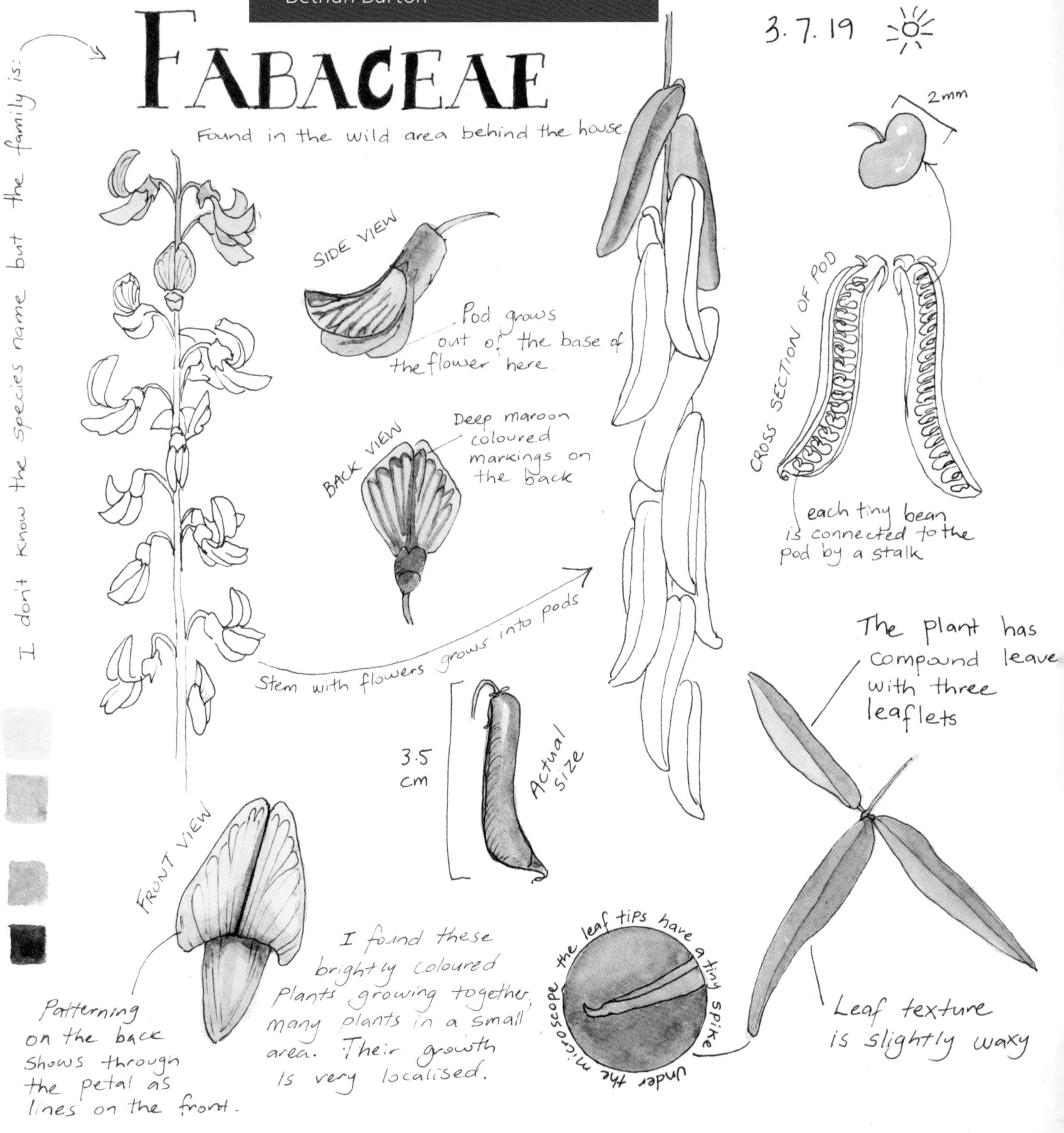

I don't know the species name but the family is:
FABACEAE
3.7.19
Found in the wild area behind the house.
SIDE VIEW
Pod grows out of the base of the flower here.
BACK VIEW
Deep maroon coloured markings on the back
Stem with flowers grows into pods
2mm
CROSS SECTION OF POD
each tiny bean is connected to the pod by a stalk
The plant has compound leaves with three leaflets
3.5 cm
Actual size
FRONT VIEW
Patterning on the back shows through the petal as lines on the front.
I found these brightly coloured plants growing together, many plants in a small area. Their growth is very localised.
Under the microscope the leaf tips have a tiny spike
Leaf texture is slightly waxy

The following text appears as handwritten notes within the nature journal illustration:

After it had foraged on the ground for a long time, vigorously lifting and tossing things aside looking for food it jumped onto a tree trunk and started doing the same

QUESTION: What is the difference between a beak and a bill? Are they the same? Is it more correct to always say bill?

The colours are so beautiful! I love the way the blend into each other on its under side.

PALE EYE WITH A STARING LOOK!

GREY/CREAM COLOURED CAP

LONG, CURVED BEAK

GREY FEATHERS AT BREAST

GREY-CROWNED

FAMILY: POMATOSTOMIDAE

Would pick up bark and leaves and move them aside

Sometimes found an insect to eat and gobbled it down before starting again

Took so many postures!

The bird was alone today, which is unusual. Normally, I see these birds in large, noisy groups. Why was this one by itself?

Spent a long time actively foraging on the ground

White tail tips

Brown Wings

Mixed brown on underside

I have often seen these birds in very large groups, foraging on the ground. It was fun to watch this individual closely. It wasn't disturbed at all by our presence. It was busy with finding its meal.

BABBLER

Pomatostomus temporalis

"I do not see myself as a very sophisticated artist. What I bring to journaling is my love and wild enthusiasm." That passionate energy also led her to establish International Nature Journaling Week, which takes place every June.

In many of her workshops, Bethan focuses on the reluctant artist. The main component of her work is helping participants break out of that feeling and open up to the experience. For example, during her podcast interviews, she always inquires about her guests' early nature experience, because she believes that nature experiences, because exposure in childhood connects us to nature for a lifetime. Her own early nature experiences were preserved by her father, who recently stumbled across a nature sketchbook Bethann had made when she was very small and shared it with her. The simple sincerity of those early sketches drove home to her how nature has impacted her life from the beginning.

As a result, Bethan is passionate about fostering a journaling practice in children. "One day when I was journaling on the front lawn with my four-year-old son, he spontaneously exclaimed with wonder in his voice, 'I didn't know that grass was so beautiful!' He is seeing things that people don't normally see. All we usually see is labels for things we have seen before. When you start to take it all in, you have an authentic heart experience."

Go Outside

Bethan emphasizes that nature journaling does not require any sort of art background or particular skills. "All you need is something to make marks *with* and something to make marks *on*. Just a piece of paper and a pencil. Go outside and look around. Start practicing intentional curiosity." When we start to pay attention to what is around us, our curiosity is piqued and our senses are engaged. Instead of rushing through the day, we become aware and tuned in to our surroundings.

Note that a nature journal is not limited to images. It can include words, numbers, and notes about your experiences. "Start to use words, pictures, and numbers in any way that feels good. You can write about what you are seeing, sketch what you see around you, or you can start to count or measure what you are seeing, which can bring another dimension to your journaling. Step outside with eyes open and start making marks to connect with and capture your environment."

Bethan Burton is an artist and environmental educator from Brisbane, Australia. She holds a bachelor of science in ecology and conservation biology and a master of environment, majoring in education for sustainability. She teaches nature journaling to all age groups and is passionate about connecting people with the natural world. Bethan is the founder of International Nature Journaling Week, an event designed to celebrate nature journaling and bring people together as a worldwide community with a shared passion. She also is the host of the *Journaling with Nature* podcast, a show that explores the joys of nature journaling through interviews with nature lovers from around the world.

To get started, go outside, open your sketchbook, or grab a piece of paper and pencil. Always add the date and location, and maybe add the time. Write some notes about how the sky looks, which will also help you get started. Bethan loves to sketch a little skyscape to begin her journaling. "If you scribble down a cloud and you have taken the time to notice details about the cloud and have noticed nature in some way, then that is a win."

That initial sketch will give you a weather stamp for that day. "Skies are important because they are accessible to anyone. It's easy to talk about the exotic, but you don't need a glamorous or unique setting. "Everyone has access to the sky. Connecting with the sky is wonderful for that reason. Many people with disabilities can't go outside, but they can usually still look out a window and connect with the sky." Start there and then begin to draw other details you see around you."

Bethan clearly possesses a warm and loving spirit. She shared this heartfelt sentiment just before we parted: "Nature journaling is not a method for improving creative skills. Rather, it is a path for connecting with your surroundings and increasing awareness of the profound beauty in the breathtaking world around us."

James Brunt
RELEASING OUTCOMES

Nature teaches us simplicity and contentment because in its presence we realize we need very little to be happy.

—*Mark Coleman*

Beech leaves, Anston Stones Wood, November 2017

James Brunt started life in South Yorkshire, in a region of the United Kingdom marked by heavy industry. He hails from a family that has worked in the mining and manufacturing industries for generations.

According to James, "Area families grew up through that system and did what their fathers and grandfathers did." James's natural career path seemed like a forgone conclusion to everyone—except James himself.

Although there are a few connections to art in the area, the largest museums are the aircraft, transport, and heritage museums. Still, James wanted to try art school.

It was a struggle, but his determination ultimately led the way to the Byam Shaw School of Art in London. "I started college as a painter and came out as an installation artist. But I couldn't find meaningful work. I was influenced by the art scene at the time, but nothing really hit me and spoke to me." Fast forward twenty years. James had been working supporting galleries and other artists and installing exhibitions, working jobs that danced along the edge of the arts world. At last, it became obvious to him that he needed to focus back on his own artwork. But after so long, it felt like he was doing a hard reboot on his life direction.

"I needed to pursue my own making. I have always loved being outdoors in nature, whether in woodland or on a beach. A few happy accidents helped me see how I could combine these things." One of those happy accidents occurred during a beach walk, when he caught a glimpse of a figure in the distance, arranging and stacking stones. "I tried to approach him, but he was cagey and secretive about it. He wanted to maintain the mystery. Still, that chance experience helped me get started." James liked the tiny, fragile connection that the mystery beach installation artist made between two rocks, but it was too myopic for him. So he started to do work that was more expansive, utilizing space and natural materials in new ways. However, even now, James still loves a bleak coastline. "It presents challenges such as the old dead matter. I enjoy working with a decaying landscape."

He kept following what the lessons on the beach taught him. "I didn't want to think too much about the process. These days I just start a repetition of pattern or texture, then follow it through. There is no stopping to plan in a structured way; I just let it evolve. I can spend hours and hours being immersed." James's state of flow provides a sense of seamless connection between himself and the surroundings. Time feels like it has slowed down, and senses become heightened. James relishes the time, often pausing to soak up his surroundings. "I may stop momentarily to watch a jaybird. Occasionally, they stroll right up to me because I have been there for hours." How breathtaking to find that, in those moments, nature views James as an integrated member of the natural environment.

Part of a global community of creatives, including several high-profile artists on social media who make similar work, James is quick to mention that his creative roots are original. He does not change the natural environment in a way that will leave it damaged or permanently altered. It has been a personal journey building this creative path. "I am very careful with the environment. The decisions I have made are borne out of learned experience, based on environmental impact, not in response to others." Another evolving original aspect of

While I work, there is no stopping to think about strategy. I enjoy just letting it evolve. By doing that, I can spend hours and hours being immersed. Instead of mindfulness, I think of it as mindlessness. I think the two are the same.

—James Brunt

Left: Deconstruction in progress, Filey Bay, January 2018

Above: Natural DNA

35

James's art is that he does not clear a space to build a natural "framework" outside for the purpose of spotlighting what he makes. Instead, when he sees the right setting, he builds *within* it. He works along with the space and sees the space as a partner, not something to dominate.

James actively maintains awareness of his environment as he strolls through the woods, which helps him discover new spaces for art, in spite of having passed the same space hundreds of times before. But even something as simple as new leaves falling from a favorite tree in his routine walk may cause him to pause and see a space that is ready to hold one of his creative statements. That's when he begins the intuitive process of building one of his delicate, sophisticated installations. "My studio *is* the woods, just a two-minute walk from my house. Many small areas under the forest canopy present themselves to me at seemingly random places and times. But I may not realize what they have to offer until I happen to see them in a moment when something random happens or there has been a natural change in the trail, and nature provides a spot."

His drive to make that temporary arrangement from nature simply kicks in. He interacts with it, becomes part of it, not working against the natural environment or imposing his own creative strategies on it. "I don't want to work against nature in terms of my creative process, which is why concentric spirals and circles reoccur a lot. I often get asked about repetition and how I keep making works that look similar." To James, none of them seem similar to each other. "Often, any kind of progression is a natural process. I'll see something really lovely that is working."

His workshops with groups help people step back from their daily lives. "I consider myself a professional child, a term coined by an artist friend of mine, but it rings so true, as I see what I do as play, and I try to help others remember to think in those imaginative, free ways that children do."

James also hosts programs in public schools that foster kids' creativity, using natural materials as a catalyst. He considers this work a two-way learning process. He loves that he can go into a setting, armed with his knowledge and a cache of materials, and, when he presents them to the kids, they often take them in completely surprising directions. He also runs a forest school, which is an educational experience based on a Danish approach to education. Forest school is a child-centered inspirational learning process that offers opportunities for holistic growth through regular sessions. It is a long-term program that supports play, exploration, and supported risk-taking. It develops confidence and self-esteem through learner-inspired, hands-on experiences in a natural setting.[1]

James is a certified forest school practitioner and has seen that the consistent experience of spending time in the forest has a powerful impact on the kids. "I take a small group of children who would struggle in academics, and provide them with regular access to natural spaces. In terms of curriculum, it's very childlike. I help them find that journey in nature. As the teacher, I am there as a facilitator for nature, just keeping them safe and helping them to move ahead in the woods, developing an understanding of risk and other key life skills."

James's humility is part of what he brings to his work and, even more importantly, to his work with other artists and groups. "I don't think I create anything in terms of artistic skill. Anyone could do what I do; they just need to give themselves the time and space to do it. It's convincing them that there's nothing stopping them from doing it. I invite people to break down those barriers themselves and play.

"I've always said that the outcome is not valuable. The experience is the real positivity for my happiness and well-being. For life, really." The idea of building a legacy directly based on his artwork is more of a necessity than a goal for James. In the case of his temporal work, that legacy takes the form of prints that people purchase. However, the true legacy that James values most is the one he is building with all the group workshops, the classroom events, and the Forest School.

Right, top to bottom:
The moment when nature reclaims
Cherry blossom, April 2019
Working on Filey Beach, the ultimate
backdrop

Go Outside

James encourages us to make a connection with place and lose ourselves in a process while outside. He feels that we do not need any particular creative or technical skills, and he encourages action versus skills development. "A lot of people think it's intricate or complex to build things in nature, but if you just start, the piece of work itself will naturally evolve."

Embrace the mindfulness/mindlessness that James advocates and you will find that your mind allows time to slip away and a flow experience appears. "People who join my workshops or join me when I am on a beach making an installation start to see something in the work. They see the patterns in nature. The work may appear complete, as though it had been planned, but I did not start out to make the seemingly complex piece that is in front of them. I just tapped into the process, and that became the outcome. Sometimes I don't even become aware of the full piece until I take a photo afterward."

James Brunt studied fine art at the Byam Shaw School of Art in London. After working for galleries and a long stint in various arts development roles, he now lives in Yorkshire with his family. He also comanages the arts organization Responsible Fishing UK, where he helps support forest education and various group creativity projects in nature. He works extensively across the UK both on his own creative journey and on delivering creative experiences for children and families. He passionately hopes that his work encourages others to find and develop their own relationship with the natural world, finding calm and peace in a fast-flowing world.

Left to right: Garden Art, 2021 | In process, working with children from Todwick Primary School | Foxy has been a regular "artist assistant" during much of James Brunt's journey. | Beach creation in progress, Sandilands Beach, South Australia

Judith Content
COLOR TOURIST

Like haiku, my work explores the essence
of an image, memory, or moment in time.
I find inspiration in nature's landscapes,
from coastal marshes to desert canyons.
Just as haiku have different interpretations,
I hope the meditative quality of my work
encourages viewers to draw upon their
own memories and experiences when
contemplating my work.

—*Judith Content*

Ephemeral installation, San Mateo Coastal Access, California, 2021

Judith Content typically works in textiles, with an occasional welcomed detour to other mediums, which she explores whenever a material or concept inspires her to take a fresh direction.

However, no matter what medium she is working in or type of project, the genesis of Judith's work is C-O-L-O-R. Early in her careet, Judith was initially fueled by the excitement of the wearable-art movement of the 1980s.

Then, when there was a building boom in her area, she was able to make several large-scale, site-specific installations. Right around 1990 that business model crashed, and that is when she started to do her own work. Today, Judith is most well known for her wall work, where she utilizes a combination of the classic kimono form and *arashi shibori* techniques.

Growing up in Massachusetts, Judith's love of the salt marshes along the Cape Cod shoreline had an impact on her as a child. That reverence for the blurred line between land and ocean continued when she moved to California in the early '70s, where she still resides. Her home in Palo Alto is near her muse, Baylands Preserve, one of the largest tracts of undisturbed marshland remaining in the San Francisco Bay area. Judith's inspiration often comes from spending time hiking the 15 miles of trails and boardwalk there, soaking in the landscape that is a result of brackish water along a mixture of tidal and freshwater habitats in the coastal California tributaries. Her response to this dramatic, misty environment has resulted in several wall pieces that reflect sheets of rain and drifts of fog. "When the fog descends, the imagery looks like the inside of an abalone shell." Everywhere she travels, Judith strives to find these moments of transcendence, and they have consistently informed her creative work.

Judith also is fortunate to live near the foothills of the Santa Cruz Mountains and regularly spends time there,

hiking through the majestic redwoods and oak chaparral and walking along the regional beaches.

Judith's chosen medium is *arashi shibori*, a type of resist-dyeing technique. The dynamic results of *arashi*, which literally means "storm" in Japanese, can be interpreted as sheets of wind and rain. She starts her process by planning a color palette. Then she wraps intricately pleated silk around a pole and secures it with threads all around. The pleats and the thread itself block the dye, creating a resist. Once she has dipped and poured the desired color palette over the pole, she unwraps it to reveal the alchemy that has taken place. "Every pole that I dye leads me to another one. Something happens with it that leads me to what I want to do next." Judith is spontaneous and doesn't try to impose too much control on the process. Unlike many artists who carefully index and record their dye experiments, Judith is instinctive. She doesn't take notes or record the results but allows each dye session to enlighten the next one. "I add and subtract colors in layers, and although I can control the results to a great extent, the element of surprise when the designs are revealed never fails to excite me."

Once the dyeing process is complete, she moves on to piecing, composition, designing, and finding the expression that the piece will convey. Judith's work is serendipitous and relies on her intuition, a trait that is demonstrated in the piece *Fire Season*, which so emotionally portrays the recent fires in California, with drifting, charred leaves flanked by the searing reds of the flames.

If we were to slip into Judith's studio during the early stages of the layout process, we would find a riot of colorful

New shapes and shadows are lingering in my mind; I'm hoping to bring them into the here and now.

—Judith Content

With the flow of the stream
I walk
and pause.
By Ozaki Hosai

Shinrin yoku: The Japanese practice of "bathing" in the atmosphere of the forest. It includes intentionally experiencing one's natural surroundings with all the senses. *Shinrin yoku* is literally translated as "forest bathing." It supports general physical and mental well-being. The focus is on the mental health benefits of immersing oneself in the natural world and letting mood guide activity.

silks strewn on the studio floor, torn up, and arranged, only to be rearranged later. She may group pieces on the design wall or floor, then leave them when she is satisfied, only to return hours or days later to discover that the arrangement needs another slice of color inserted in exactly the right spot to complete the composition. She keeps rolling with this process until the combination consistently resonates with her, and she is ready to move to the next stage. Judith uses the sewing machine to draw lines and strokes, like strokes of a paintbrush, to highlight the movement and flow of the piece. "The composition of fragments is meticulously secured to the design wall, studied, refined, and finally sewn together. Then, the actual quilting on the surface defines portions of the design, and appliqué is often applied to accentuate depth or movement in the piece."

Judith often describes her work as a metaphor for Japanese haiku—short, unrhymed poems associated with brief, suggestive imagery intending to evoke emotion. "Like haiku, my work explores the essence of an image, memory, or moment in time. I find inspiration in nature's landscapes, from coastal marshes to desert canyons. Just as haiku have different interpretations, I hope the meditative quality of my work encourages viewers to draw upon their own memories and experiences when contemplating my work."

Judith's embrace of the ephemeral has allowed her to celebrate her passion for color in many contexts. She calls herself a color tourist. A driving force in her life is the quest for stunning color experiences. One such discovery was a trip to Crater Lake in south-central Oregon, famous for its deep-blue color and water clarity that

inspires awe. Indigenous Americans witnessed its formation 7,700 years ago, when a violent volcanic eruption triggered the collapse of a tall peak. Scientists marvel at the lake's purity. Fed by rain and snow, it is the deepest lake in the United States and one of the most pristine on earth. "I walked up to Crater Lake in Oregon and burst into tears. The lake is so deep [that] the longer wavelengths, red, orange, yellow, and green, are absorbed. The scattered blue light is redirected back to the surface as a color unlike anything you have ever seen."

An invitation from the Palo Alto Arts Center in 2009 gave Judith the opportunity to step outside her typical color-focused textile work. She was invited to create an installation that welcomes guests to the Arts Center. She responded to the request with *Pottery Creek*, an undulating, multicolored, sculptural creek that runs along both sides as guests approach the Art Center. As part of the process, community members collected ceramics and delivered them to a local community center, which she collected weekly for several months. She then took the pieces home, broke them into even smaller fragments, and softened their edges in a tumbler that she ran twenty-four hours a day until she had ultimately tumbled 4,000 pounds of ceramics! "People interact with it, some pick up and move the pieces, and I love all of that. I occasionally add more pieces to the installation and keep the creek flowing." Judith took pleasure in the irony of this project. As a lifelong beachcomber who relishes carefully finding and collecting treasures, she relished pouring out the treasures this time and arranging them in the landscape for others to find.

A smaller version of *Pottery Creek* was later included in

47

a one-woman show at the San Jose Museum of Quilts and Textiles in 2019. She titled this show *Evanescence*, which highlights the impermanence of the subjects of her work . . . fleeting or vanishing quickly, vanishing like vapor.

While her wall works are still an anchor, a recent tangent has taken Judith into site-specific, ephemeral land art. During the pandemic, she dove into her cache of *shibori*-dyed silks and, inspired by Japanese *sashiko* stitching, created mushroom forms perched on bamboo stakes. From a technical standpoint, she is now making many complex forms out of heavy archival watercolor paper. "The paper can be manipulated, so it was an engineering challenge." She cuts, slits, and manipulates them, then figures out how to stretch the fabric over the paper forms and stitch the surface. "There are several factors involved. If you include padding, you get undulating forms. If not, they are sharp-edged forms. The effects vary." Each silk sculpture is made from her scraps and therefore is imbued with a backstory related to previous pieces.

Judith has hauled these sculptures out to wild spaces to experiment with how they respond in different settings. She started by lining them up along the outcroppings at Asilomar Beach in Pacific Grove, California. Once they were set up, Judith could tell that there was something to be explored. "They are reminiscent of sea life. They could be imaginary sea life. But if they are installed up in the hills, they can look like mushrooms on the woodland floor."

The first installation was along the wrack line, where organic material such as kelp and seagrass are cast up onto the beach by surf, tides, and wind.

Judith intends to pursue her idea of making a large-scale installation from these ephemeral sculptures. She would love to fill a gallery space with this new work. "I would like to display so many of them together in a space where you could walk underneath them or look down on them, filling the space, making the color gradations spill across the room." Judith has already made four hundred of these itinerant sculptures that foster fleeting installations, so she can explore how they look when installed en masse. "So often, I am creating work for an upcoming exhibition, and this time I don't have one; I'm just making the work anyway. It's so freeing."

When the sculptures are installed in their various habitats, they seem to take up residence and enhance whatever environment they are placed in, whether that is on the beach, along the forest floor, or perched in the opening of burned-out tree stumps. Judith remarked, "They don't conflict with their environment. They move in and feel like they were always there." Judith has been known to hike two or three hours with a custom backpack that she designed herself to hold the pieces. When she finds the right place, she installs them. It takes a couple of hours to complete the installation, and time stops while she completes the quiet, meditative process. Once she is done, she photographs the entire scene before packing them up again and hiking out. "The process itself makes time stand still for me. There are so many things to consider: the gradation of colors, the height, how they work with the environment. It's euphoric."

The next time she goes out, the same sculptures will be regrouped according to colors and texture, then

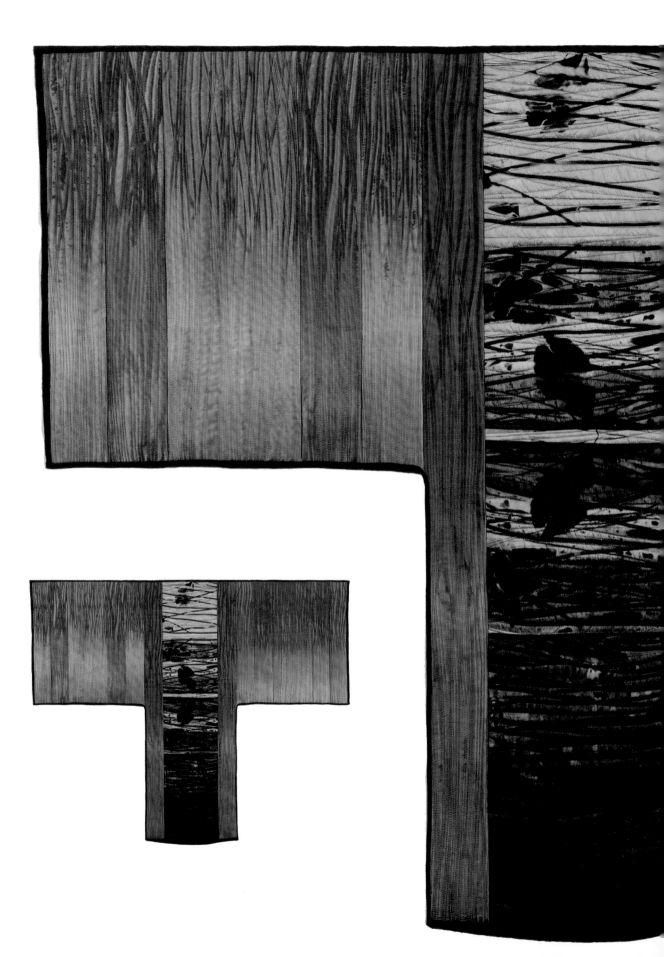

There are no lines in nature, only areas of color, one against another.

—Edouard Manet

Opposite: Ephemeral installation, Carmel State Beach, California, 2020

Below left: Studio, work table, preparing a wall piece to quilt

reinstalled in a new location. "They may be on white sand, against the rocks and shore, or along the line where the fires met the ocean. The complex set of fires that ravaged the Santa Cruz Mountains in 2020 have left blackened, stark land and trees set against the shore, barren of vegetation. I think the fire almost cooked the soil there. I have also installed them up in the hills against the green grass, which will change to yellow as it dries out, so I'm looking forward to trying that out."

Whether it is a wall piece, mushrooms, or tumbled ceramic shards, Judith's work is based on bringing many pieces together to make a whole. Her wall pieces were originally composed of small fabric scraps, so they naturally came together in a collage format. "Pulling back

to a wider view, having all of these pieces gives you all sorts of ways to assemble things, by texture, color, and any other elements. If I had a huge canvas in front of me, I wouldn't know where to start. But if I paint all these other elements and put them together, that feels like a world of possibilities. I think that things come together in a richer form when things are put together and combined. They are juxtaposed; there is a vibration; they meld together in a particular way."

"People see different things in my work because of their own experiences in life. That is also the nature of haiku. They can be interpreted in many different ways. That is their magic. There is usually more to a haiku than you think. They too are like a collage."

Go Outside

Judith Content considers herself a color tourist and wants to share that passion with others. "I travel specifically to see color phenomenon. I react to it in a visceral way." Roussillon, France, is one such pilgrimage that Judith and her husband sought out a few years ago. The area has mountains and cliffs filled with ocher and used to be home to an ocher mine. The village of Roussillon sparkles with ocher color under the deep-blue sky because the town itself is painted in color gradations from brilliant red to gold. "We travel everywhere to find these types of places." She also seeks out humble color experiences. "It doesn't have to be a landscape that overwhelms you. It's also the subtle colors that you might see in rocks or minerals in your own area. Get outside, then slow down. Your sense of color will be heightened."

The next time you step outside, embrace Judith's passion for color and appreciate the things that are transitory in nature—the afternoon light dancing off rocks along the shore, fog drifting through a marshland area, or the sky reflected in a perfectly blue lake—to help foster gratitude and curiosity for your surroundings.

Judith Content graduated from San Francisco State University with a BA in fine art, with an emphasis in textiles. She has been a full-time studio artist for more than forty years. She exhibits in the United States and other countries, and her work is represented in museums and in public and private collections, including the Mountain View and Sunnyvale campuses of the Palo Alto Medical Foundation. She served on the Palo Alto Art Center Foundation Board, as a juror for Quilt National and Quilt Visions, and as president of Studio Art Quilt Associates (SAQA). Her work is featured in several publications. In addition to working with textiles, Content enthusiastically explores other creative paths, including jewelry design, bookmaking, collage, pottery, pottery installations, and more.

Left to right: Sheer cliff face, Roussillon, France | 2016, 48 × 75 inches | Studio, work table, wild mushrooms, in progress

Nick Neddo
GUIDED BY THE EARTH

For me, it all ties back to a love of nature, starting from growing up in Vermont and having access to beautiful wild places, finding my sense of stability, adventure, and awe-inspiring moments of life when I have been blown away by the beauty. That's given me a deep love and respect for the environment.

—*Nick Neddo*

One of the running themes of Nick Neddo's work as an artist is the witnessing of special, everyday moments. One might not think of a bear and a hummingbird having a conversation as normal, but how much of a bear's or hummingbird's daily life have you actually observed? Nature is constantly in dynamic dialogue.

I first met Nick Neddo several years ago as part of an interview for a magazine story, at a time when the idea for *Create Naturally* was still just a vague thought in the back of my mind.

The story was intended to focus on his basketmaking techniques, and while they are impressive, they represent only one arrow in Nick's overflowing quiver. Wife and new baby notwithstanding, His original life partner is unquestionably the natural landscape around him. At the core, Nick's identity is the natural byproduct of the relationship between his surroundings and the areas of expertise that he has developed throughout his life. "It all started as a question: 'If I lived in the Stone Age, would I still consider myself an artist?'

I realized that the answer is yes because that is how I identify with the world and interact with it. The next question that followed was 'What would that look like?' That really launched me into this ongoing thought experiment that ventured beyond thought and into the physical world with my hands."

What Nick once thought would be a lark has evolved into the central theme of his life. However, labeling him as solely an artist would drastically oversimplify the layers of activities he engages in. When asked, Nick describes himself as an inventor, experimenter, experimental archeologist, mistake maker, and learner. He has spent years honing survival and ancient-technology abilities in many areas, which ultimately laid the foundation for the artwork that he creates. Unlike most artists, he begins by harvesting and making all of his own supplies and tools. His made-by-hand materials all have started with foraging while wandering in the woods. They include charcoal drawing sticks, crayons, inks, pens, paints, paintbrushes, printmaking tools, handmade paper, sketchbooks, ceramic inkwells, and paint dishes. In his words, "The material is art itself, wild-crafted from the landscape."

The expansive line of thought that pervades Nick's life is his ongoing contemplation of his place in the world and in time. "I get an extra tingle of excitement or sense of purpose while I'm in the creative process, almost as if I'm stepping back into a continuum of a creative lineage." In other words, we are simply playing our role in this generation, and we are part of an important lineage of humans, all of whom have used their ancestral abilities to experience, create, and savor the world around them. For Nick, this line of thought is freeing. When he is frustrated or stuck, he pauses to look at the bigger picture to regain composure and context. "We are stepping into a river for just this moment. How do we want to spend that?"

Nick's traditional ecological knowledge base includes land art creations that serve humans and wildlife, basketmaking, stone cutting, bow-and-arrow making, hunting, living off the land, and creating his art, all completely sourced from the environment around him. Nick's mastery of the outdoors serves as the base for all of the creative work that he is known for in the fine-craft-and-art world. Many people who admire his creations likely do not realize that Nick laid this foundation of learning and living in ways that our ancestors lived well before he started making art.

Recently, the term "primitive skills" has gained popularity on social media. When asked about that, Nick is ambivalent. With a slight cringe, he remarked that this fad has been interesting, but his concern is that many

56

Every man is a quotation from all his ancestors.

—Ralph Waldo Emerson

"I like to watch things grow. And I like to sit in verdant spaces slightly hidden, unobtrusively watching the shadows crawl across the landscape. This dome provides such an opportunity and marks the beginning of an exciting angle of my 'living sculptural spaces' project."

"My 'studio' is really just anywhere I set myself up when I feel inspired to be creative. I like to think of those fleeting moments as being visited by a special friend, the Muse, who comes only when she wants, and whose company is an invitation to do some magic. This is the indoor space that I have set aside to invite that elusive visitor."

"I make my crayons from earth pigments with beeswax as the binder. Without the bees, I would just have piles of colorful powdered soil. So, as is a theme in my more recent work, I feature the creatures that offer the material gifts that make the handmade medium possible."

people are attracted to the *idea* of primitive skills but do not explore them further for themselves. In those cases, his stance is that they are missing the meaning and are forgoing the riches that these core abilities provide. He would be heartened to see more people authentically embrace their own relationship to the earth.

"Ancestral skills take on importance because I am continually reaching to the past to build context for the present and future, building a place for myself." Nick feels that most of the existential problems we experience originate in our disconnect from nature and the loss of our ancestors' knowledge. "Reaching back to our common ancestry, we all have Indigenous heritage, depending on how far back we look. It is a bridge back to our Stone Age past and the wisdom that I find inherent there. We are all the same *Homo sapiens* and have the same creative prowess and ingenuity. I also gain a lot of satisfaction from making things, fashioning raw materials into functional tools that can contribute to wilderness survival—and also just daily life."

Nick's life is driven by a sense of purpose and self-discovery. He relies on a childlike satisfaction and exploration and an ongoing sense of experimentation, especially in regard to making his own art supplies from scratch. "In the process of learning how to make any particular thing, such as a basket, a water bottle, or a stone tool, you need to learn about materials, locations, times to locate, how to process them, and your hands have to actually learn how to work with them. That process is an invitation to continue going deeper into the earth, and deeper into our ancestry."

Although Nick sees our current spot in the geologic process as a slow march to global obsolescence, he gains peace of mind by knowing that cycles happen with life in general, and that "humanity is a tiny, young species." Environmental trauma is a condition formed from the knowledge that our activities are literally changing the course of the earth's evolution and finding it increasingly difficult to psychologically mediate the results of our actions. Nick's attitude helps us put environmental trauma into perspective. Instead of feeling hopeless, he embraces the longer perspective on our global environmental problems. "Honestly, that way of thinking does help me give myself permission to be fully immersed in the creative process. What else are we here for? To be in the moment and be participants in our own lives."

In the midst of all his creative activities, including publishing books on his art making, Nick is aware that many people are not aware of his extensive training in nature before any of his books were published. Those pursuits have a wide reach but represent fairly recent projects. "The thing people may not fully understand is that there were twenty years before that of immersing myself into ancestral skills and wilderness survival skills, nature survival skills. I taught primitive technology and wilderness survival skills for all those years before these books came out. That is still very much a part of my creative process and is still very relevant to me, as an instructor and a lifelong student." Nick also continues to study Paleolithic and other Stone Age ancient technologies. Essentially, his art is comfortably nested within a life that is intensely focused on the outdoors. "It is a marriage between the guiding pursuits of my life, which are visual arts, and the parallel and sometimes competing pursuit of wilderness skills, such as tracking, building shelter, fire, finding water, food, making bows and arrows, and primitive hunting and fishing techniques."

Top left: As with much of Neddo's land art works, the vision of the future form compels him into a relationship of annual tending and continuing the work in stages. In many cases, the work evolves through the process of decay. Other times, the work literally grows as it takes on a life of its own.

Bottom left: "This form just appeared in my mind's eye one night as I lay drifting off to sleep. Somewhere in that liminal zone between awake and asleep, I was there, standing next to this elliptical earthen form."

"A painting, like a photograph, can be a moment frozen in time. I made this painting with pigments ground directly from stones. It is recognition of another kind of moment when time stands still."

Go Outside

Nick's advice is to try to learn from the earth itself, which requires spending regular, quiet time with the landscape in a conversational manner. "Most importantly, a conversation is also listening, not just talking. So, it's important to pay attention to all we see and hear as part of that 'conversation.' For example, I suggest going on a quest or a wander. You hold a question in your mind, walk the landscape, and broadcast your intent to learn or be more informed. Especially in the natural world, our dominant paradigm does not leave much room for other creatures and nature. When I want to learn something, I do not always have access to human teachers. Even if I did, they may not know what I want to know. So, I go directly to the earth. The teachers themselves learned how to participate in the landscape in the same ways that stealthy wild animals do, and that requires a lot of time spent in nature itself."

Nick Neddo is a sixth-generation Vermonter who has been making art since he could pick up a crayon. He grew up exploring the wetlands, forests, and fields of his bioregion and developed a profound curiosity, respect, and love for the community of life around him. As a youngster, Nick identified his main areas of interest that would become lifelong pursuits: study of the natural world, Stone Age technology (popularly known as primitive skills), and creating art. Trusting the inherent value of these skills, he continues to embrace their pursuit with a ravenous appetite fueled by a genuine love of the living world and the creative process.

Left to right: Sheets of paper made from found natural materials | Hummus Park Land Art piece | Harvesting willow for baskets | Nick's handmade paintbrushes

Nick reminds us that nature is a conscious entity that has things to teach us—if we ask. He encourages letting go of defined processes, sitting with your own boredom, and listening to the ideas that float to the surface of your mind. You may even add doodling into the mix. Take paper and pencil along for the ride. Start simply, make patterns, and be in the flow. Nick said, "There is so much room for a reboot from the benefits of doodling. It takes intentionality to open the mind space. I see myself as a cocollaborator with the elements, with weather, and time. We take turns adding our touch. One of these days, I look forward to seeing mushrooms sprouting out of this dancing wall of wood."

Jan Hopkins
CONTAINING NATURE

Everything in nature is such a wonder.
Even when you see tiny bugs or spiders
clustered together on a web. If you tap the
web, they all come together in a little
webbed ball of protection. It's all so
fascinating. It is the wonder of the creation
in general, and what a miracle in general
life is. How do you capture that?

—*Jan Hopkins*

Minerva—2004, 20 × 17 × 9 inches. Materials cherry bark, Alaskan yellow cedar, and waxed linen. Exhibited at
SOFA Expo, Chicago, 2004. *Photo: ©2004 Wendy McEahern Photography, private collection*

Jan Hopkins is a storyteller who is deeply connected to her family history and handwork of indigenous cultures.

While she is known for sculptural vessels, her work takes many forms and is built on a background palette of unique materials.

The first time I stood in front of Jan's work was more than a decade ago. It was *Fish Out of Water*, a sculpture formed in the idealized female form, created with sturgeon skin, halibut skin, salmon skin, waxed linen, bull kelp, ostrich shell beads, and shell buttons. What struck me then—and it still holds true now—is that her work is equal parts surprising materials and intuitive storytelling. Her exclusive use of materials harvested from nature provides a gateway for inquiry about the narrative that she wants to share. Many artists have a backstory of being a maker from birth, an "inner knowing" of sorts. Jan has a different and unexpected narrative.

Her art career started on a hot afternoon when she stopped by the Heard Museum in Phoenix, Arizona, one of the world's preeminent museums for the presentation, interpretation, and advancement of American Indian art. The Heard Museum is known for emphasizing the intersection of Native American art with broader artistic and cultural themes. Most importantly for Jan, this was the first time that she had encountered baskets made by Indigenous peoples. That experience sparked a sea change in her life. She found herself overwhelmed by the sincerity, creativity, and cultural implications of the exhibition. She gained a reverence for the artists and the stories behind each basket.

The quiet but growing storm within Jan was further helped along by her tenacity. But wandering through the museum on that day brought her creative stirrings together with her own background, and her life has not been the same since. From that day, she has spent her life making work that explores her own heritage and connects her with her passion for learning about Indigenous cultures around the world.

In 1988, Jan was given the opportunity to start classes at a local basketry school in the Seattle, Washington, area. She started by learning Appalachian basketry techniques and ultimately took every available workshop. She also tried working with several different kinds of materials but always found herself returning to nature-based materials. "I couldn't foster an interest in recycled materials, upcycling, metals, or plastics. Even now, I always come back to materials that are harvested in nature."

Jan feels a deep connection to Indigenous makers. She is a second-generation Japanese American, and her own family history reflects a narrative of displacement, survival, taking root, and ultimately thriving in an adverse situation. Jan grew up in Idaho, near Minidoka, a World War II Japanese American prison center where her parents, grandparents, aunts, and uncles all were assigned to live. At the end of the war, they were each given twenty-five dollars and released to restart their lives. This seed money was intended to facilitate travel back to their home state and to help them rebuild their lives. However, Jan's parents ended up settling on a farm in Idaho. Throughout her childhood, her American heritage was emphasized, and she was not taught anything about her Japanese heritage, for fear of social retribution. "A lot of people my age didn't know they were Japanese and had no knowledge of their own cultural background

Our bodies are containers that hold our stories.

—John McQueen

leaves

agave leaves
eucalyptus leaves
smoke tree leaves
blackberry leaves
ginkgo leaves
big-leaf maple
philodendron leaves
skeleton leaves
laurel leaves
maple leaves
tulip tree leaves
hydrangea leaves

fruit peels

Meyer lemon peels
orange peels
watermelon peels
grapefruit peels
pomegranate peels
cantaloupe peels
canary melon peels
mandarin peels

barks & branches

yellow cedar bark
red cedar bark
cherry bark
birch bark
black bamboo
concord grapevines
palm seed stalk branches

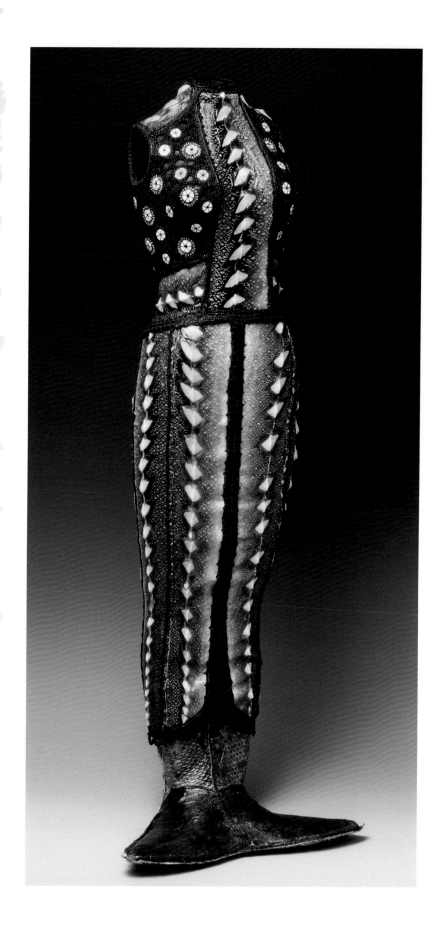

Left: Fish Out of Water—2010, 31½ × 11½ × 7 inches. Materials: sturgeon skin, halibut skin, salmon skin, waxed linen, bull kelp, ostrich shell beads, and shell buttons. *Photo: Ken Rowe, private collection*

because their parents were so afraid and wanted us to be Americans. They didn't want to show any hint of being Japanese because of what had happened to them."

Much of Jan's work explores the narratives around this complex family history. She is currently working on a piece that explores the compelling backstory of a cousin who was protected from the internment experience by obtaining a falsified birth certificate, giving her a Hispanic heritage. She lived her entire life without going back to her original Japanese identity, leaving her children without any knowledge of their heritage. In this piece and in all of her work, Jan is focused on two things: the power of the narrative that is conveyed, and the visual materials that make the most sense for that piece.

Jan is creating work for a two-person exhibition with her husband, Chris, at the Bainbridge Island Museum of Art in Washington State that will memorialize the eightieth anniversary of the first group of Japanese people who were sent to an internment camp. Each piece tells a unique life story. For example, her grandfather was part of a samurai family, and she is developing a piece that tells his story of immigrating to the United States with great hopes of the American dream. Through much adversity, he was successful through the Great Depression. And he was well respected among the Japanese people. Tragically, the war broke him, and he was never the same afterward. "He was part of a samurai family. His ancestral family sword was confiscated and never returned to the family after the war." Jan is dedicated to telling these stories and is careful to point out that even though these are her own family's stories, they represent the experiences many families endured during that time.

Since that initial experience at Heard Museum more than thirty years ago, Jan's work has been carried along on a current of Indigenous influences and firsthand experiences from around the world. She has traveled to the Oceania region, meeting, learning from, and sharing with Maori artists and teachers in New Zealand. She discovered during a visit to Australia that she had been practicing a traditional looping technique used by the Australian Aboriginals for thousands of years.

All these relationships and adventures have circled back to the power of story expressed in a visual medium. For example, in Native basketry, patterns may express the landscape, capture an event in time, tell a story, or reveal the cultural connections of the weaver. In recent years, Jan also has been involved with activities at the Native Longhouse (*Wharenui* in the Maori language) and Cultural Center, on the Indigenous Arts campus of Evergreen College in Olympia, Washington. The campus includes the Longhouse, a fiber arts studio, and an old carving studio. Now there is a new carving studio, and a cast-glass studio is in the works. Jan has attended several international gatherings there and has been able to learn about the Indigenous carvings and other Native hand skills, all of which have enriched her own creative work.

Jan continued to improve her technical skills through the years, parallel to her abiding passion for indigenous cultures. She had taken every basketry technique class that she could find, and was moving with great purpose toward mastery. Then a remark by a friend of hers, artist John McQueen, gave her pause. He said, "Maybe you know too much." John encouraged her to let go of her preconceived ideas about her work. From that moment, she realized that she could combine all parts of herself to refine her vision. "I thought, 'John is right!' I am depending too much on my technique and not my instinct." That was a watershed moment for Jan. "I realized at that point that I didn't need to incorporate all that I had learned." This turning point freed her to use materials and techniques together in much more creative ways.

"I began to concentrate on the design in my head, and that's what I needed to do. I had to come up with other ways to construct, to preserve the natural beauty of the materials, so they maintained their innocence. It gives you delight to see things you recognize from nature. That was my thinking. Then I started bringing in the materials as part of the symbology of the piece." One example is agave, which is regularly stripped and cut down in the process of being mined for its natural

(u-nig mu)—2005, 39 × 13 × 10 inches. *Technique:* interior vessel molded silver dollar pods of man's faceless head, with a mask floating above the head. Interior lined with weathered hydrangea leaves.

sweetener. Jan wanted to find a way to sustain the beauty of the leaves, in hopes that people would recognize them and absorb the purity of Mother Nature and the materials she provides.

Jan is passionate about experimenting with interesting materials, figuring out what they can or cannot do. "I like to push and go beyond. My work is derived from tradition. Then I ask myself what else is out there that I can experiment with. If one material works, I try similar plants, skins, seeds, and anything else that comes to mind." Jan also has a unique skill for seeing the finished works in her head. She does not sketch or draw plans.

She simply goes to her studio and starts making what she has already seen in her mind's eye.

Through all of her learning and growing, and despite the fact that her work often does not look at all like our preconceived notion of the basket form, Jan still considers herself a basket maker—although sometimes the only things her baskets contain are their stories. "I feel lucky because I have been connected with such incredible people—artists, collectors, people who connect artists with one another, and people who have encouraged me to think expansively. I'm so grateful to have this life."

Reflections—the Dance, a collaboration with Chris Hopkins (painted base). 2007, 26 × 18 × 24 inches. Medium: oil painting on wood, lotus pod tops, silver dollar pods, waxed linen, and paper. Exhibited at SOFA Expo, Chicago, 2007. *Photo: Phil Howe, private collection*

Left: Cut from the Same Cloth—Banner: 54 × 32 inches; cutout figure: 28 × 14 inches, 2018. Materials: felt needle felting

Above: California poppies, Burke Gilman Trail, Seattle, Washington

fish skins

salmon skin

halibut skins

sturgeon skins

seeds, seed pods, & petals

lotus pods

devil's claw seed pods

cardiocrinum seeds

dried hydrangea flowers

weathered hydrangea petals

lunaria seed pod centers

dried artichoke

snapdragon seed pods

Chinese lantern seed pods

miscellaneous

hornet nest paper

acorn nuts

ostrich shell beads

emu egg

seaweed

bull kelp

driftwood

clamshells

rocks

concretions

nonorganic materials

cotton cloth

watch parts

beads

Go Outside

Jan lives near Puget Sound in Washington. She relishes the rugged coastline, mountains, and evergreen forests. It is easy to understand how her inspiration often comes from stories, thoughts, or ideas that occur to her while she is on walks in her area. "There is such a wonderful silence. The visuals take me to another place. I see designs while I am walking." Jan suggests taking walks like she does, and letting your mind be free during those times. She takes photos to make a record of what she sees and to remind her of the ideas that sprouted from the subjects of the photo. She captures the light, shadows, and designs that nature has to share with us. "Some of my ideas come from just the silence and being able to focus closely on one thing at a time. When you clear your mind, suddenly your thoughts also become clearer. I will do some problem-solving during my walk, and my creative challenges or even challenges I am facing in my life become clear to me."

Jan Hopkins is a master at creating sculptural vessels from unusual natural materials such as citrus peel, lotus pods, sturgeon skin, leaves, and seed pods while simultaneously incorporating traditional materials such as ostrich eggshell beads and cedar bark. Each piece is a marriage of deep sensitivity and reverence to materials, with a heavy emphasis on concept and innovation. Jan studied basketry with Indigenous and contemporary artists, learning the art of meticulous construction and the basics of how to gather and prepare materials and understand new concepts in design beyond traditional construction. An award-winning artist, Jan has exhibited nationally and internationally. Her artwork is in permanent collections, including the Fuller Craft Museum in Brockton, Massachusetts; the Museum of Art and Design in New York City; the Museum of Fine Arts in Boston; and Racine Art Museum in Racine, Wisconsin.

Jan also encourages considering almost everything around you as potential material for creation. She gathers, dries, and prepares natural materials in many ways. She is a collector of nature. Whether the items she finds on her walks become part of her future work or not, they feed her creativity.

"I want everyone to understand the creation that is out there; we step on it every day. When you start to really appreciate the colors and the surroundings, you can't help but get inspired by a simple walk in the woods or being out on the beach. Focusing on the details out there, then panning back and seeing a heron fly off into the sky. I am amazed at the drama unfolding between these two views. Like a camera, I focus, then back away and see the whole of it. It's all wonderful to me."

Meredith Woolnough
SAVORING LIFE'S FIELDWORK

The more I work with natural forms, the more I find myself drawn into the science of nature. I am fascinated by the way things are built, the way they grow and function. I often find myself marveling at the perfection of a single leaf or the phenomenal beauty of a coral reef, and it can be quite overwhelming at times, almost spiritual.

The relationship between nature and my work is cyclical. It's a virtuous circle. Life giving.

—*Meredith Woolnough*

Meredith Woolnough reveals the exquisite delicacy of nature through embroidered sketches that float above the canvas.

With only a sewing machine and palette of thread, she creates airy, light interpretations of the specimens that she studies in nature. Meredith's process begins with fieldwork. She researches the forms in nature that captivate her, and meticulously makes several drawings.

"Although it may not be necessary to take so much time with the research, it's part of the connection that I am building. If I really understand what I am depicting, I end up with a much-stronger piece." If she is studying a particular leaf, Meredith learns its exact genus and species, then uses that information to pull out the most important elements of the design and highlights those characteristics. "Although I am not interested in creating photorealistic work, the background I have developed drives my process now."

The background Meredith speaks of is her most recent degree in natural history illustration from the University of Newcastle in Australia. This is her third degree, and each one has taken her to new depths in the creative life that she has been unearthing since childhood. "I've always been an artsy person. I always painted, did ceramics. Making art has been a pervasive theme in my life."

Once she is satisfied with the botanical study of her current subject, she then enlists her sewing machine as a sketching tool to transfer her ideas to a different medium. Meredith has trained herself to discover the often-overlooked patterns in nature, enlarging the size and re-presenting them to us with her sketching-sewing process. Meredith eschews fabric backing and instead uses water-soluble stabilizer. Once she has completed the work, she soaks the piece in a bowl of warm water and, as if by magic, the stabilizer melts away, leaving only the gossamer stitching behind.

The result of Meredith's process is captivating interpretations of forms from nature that appear to occupy physical space while also being weightless and translucent.

A move from the suburbs of Sydney to coastal Newcastle a decade ago caused (quite literally) a sea change in her life. Living along the ocean opened up a world of aquatic plants and sea life that sparked even more learning and exploration in a life that had already been driven by her thirst for knowledge. "I live a couple minutes' walk from the beach, and we have lots of pockets of bushland and a reserve. I'm spoiled for natural environments. I make exploring that area part of my practice. I have a four-year-old and a nine-month-old, so right now I am fitting my art practice into my new life. I'm still committed to making my work. It's a part of who I am."

Newcastle is host to a thriving grassroots art scene, with artist-led studios and gallery spaces peppered throughout town. This environment has further inspired Meredith's creative growth. "I used to have a shared art space here, which has given me lots of connections."

Over the years, Meredith has gradually defined a process that has led to her current life of integrating creativity and learning within the creative hub of her coastal town. But she started in a very different place. Right out of high school, Meredith went to art school, untethered by any particular medium but eager to learn. "I finished high school and went straight into art school. I had no plans of being an artist full time, because it seemed lofty and impractical. I was very naive. There I

All my life through, the new sights of nature made me rejoice like a child.

—*Marie Curie*

discovered textile arts and ended up majoring in textiles by mistake because I had accidentally accrued enough units for that major. Basically, I learned many things by taking classes in every medium, but I didn't master any of them."

Meredith's first bachelor's degree included broad general art knowledge, but she was still looking for her own creative identity. "It was generally a good experience, but I didn't find the thing that grabbed me." Meredith felt like she didn't belong. She couldn't relate to all the conceptual art that was being made and was the subject of much discussion around her. She didn't feel that she was a part of it. "I was overwhelmed because I saw so many artists who concentrated on conceptual work. I felt like I was not able to be part of that conversation." Still, Meredith did well academically. She started in the textiles department, the outsider of the art school, which was housed in a nondescript back corner of the building. She completed her degree with honors. In Meredith's humble opinion, "I'm not necessarily talented; I have just worked really hard."

Then a shift happened in her life. The university gave Meredith the opportunity to do an honors year. She decided to take her sewing machine along for the ride. When the academic year began, Meredith was ready—and determined—to learn to use her sewing machine in new ways. "I even took a sewing machine into life-drawing classes, much to the chagrin of all the other students!"

During that time, she focused on trial and error, finding new ways to explore the subjects that she was "drawing" with her machine. "When I discovered water-soluble fabric, it was a new day. That was such an exciting concept. I focused that whole year on exploring it. I played, made all the mistakes.

"I wish I could approach my practice now with the same naivete and curiosity. During that year, I learned how to shape the embroidery and mold it to make it sculptural." She also learned to blend colors as a benefit of a day when she happened to have a problem with her sewing machine. "I was amazed. I learned to blend because I had the tension set all wrong on the machine. I ended up pulling so much of my bobbin thread up to the top that the colors were mixed together. I then ended up refining that and making it a mix of colors. It was earth shattering. Until then, I hated it when there were tension issues with my machine. But what a revelation! I didn't realize that thread could be mixed effectively this way."

Meredith ultimately went on to get a master's in teaching at the University of Sydney. This allowed her to become a high school textiles and design teacher. While working with high school students, she continued to do embroidery and connected with a group of artists to build a small gallery show in Paddington, a neighboring community.

As it happens, all the work for the show was small, so they named the show *Petite*. For that show, Meredith created a series of pieces representing coral. Several pieces sold. "That was pivotal for me. I realized that I was really on to something that captivated people. I had recently learned to scuba dive on the Great Barrier Reef. I made this series of nine coral pieces, all made on the same old embroidery hoop that I had been using for a long time and sewn on my worn-out sewing machine. I wanted to come up with a beautiful way to display them. I took inspiration from entomology practices—how they pinned and arranged the specimens. I experimented with pinning my pieces on boards and discovered the

Clockwise from top left: Meredith mounting her *Paper Nautilus* | Stitching a coral fan design | Stitching *Paper Nautilus*

Paper Nautilus (embroidery thread and pins on paper, 59 × 70 cm (framed size). This piece is inspired by the beautiful ribbed patterns on the *Argonauta argo*.

pieces would cast shadows, highlighting the dimensionality of the work.

Petite marked the beginning of a series of shows that continue to this day. Her work has been shown throughout Australia, the United Kingdom, and the United States and can be found in private and corporate collections.

Eventually Meredith left teaching, and that is when she went back to college and learned the core skills of botanical illustration that frame the work she makes today. "I felt that I was lacking some of the drawing skills that I needed to get the designs in my mind out of my head and onto the artwork." She had never heard of a degree concentration in natural-history illustration, but a series of serendipitous circumstances led her to the course, including a chance meeting while waiting in line at a grocery store and a chat with enthusiastic visitors at an exhibition opening. She started with the intention of taking just one class but ended up happily studying natural-history illustration for the next four years and completing another degree. "It gave me the fieldwork background that is now the foundation of my work. Before I was just working from pictures and prints. They were stylized interpretations of actual species in the natural

world. I was fascinated by the ecosystem and nature in general but lacked a sophisticated understanding. As I progressed in my studies, I gained a greater understanding of the ecosystem. Now I am so much more invested in the organisms and species." Meredith's botanical illustration education was completely unlike her art school experience from years before. "It was like going to art school without the egos. Just people who loved nature and drawing. I felt so lost and intimidated by the other art students when I attended art school after high school—just a little girl in the corner with textiles." This time, Meredith had found her tribe.

These days, Meredith spends her days making more of her signature work and sharing it with the world in exhibitions and books and by teaching workshops. "So many people connect to it; they see different things in it. I love hearing the reasons people collect my work. Recently one of my ginkgo pieces sold because the couple was under a ginkgo tree when they became engaged. So many people have connections with nature for different reasons. We all want to connect with nature. It is our first relationship."

This page: Maidenhair fern (2020) embroidery thread and pins on paper, 20 × 20 cm (framed size). Embroidery from the "100 Embroideries Project." Meredith's interpretation of maidenhair fern (*Adiantum*).

Go Outside

Meredith suggests analyzing how different things in nature relate to each other. "Nothing compares to the connection you feel when you spend time really looking at something closely and paying attention to the environment around it. "The subjects are never singular but are always connected to the environment in which they live and thrive." Learning to see is really the fundamental base of Meredith's work. She suggests that botanical illustration is where you start. "It requires research, which leads to fresh ways of interpreting what you see. The goal is not necessarily to interpret nature as accurately as possible. Rather, the goal is to have enough of an understanding of what you see to pull out the elements that will inform your work."

Left to right: This is the major series of works created during 2020 for Meredith's solo exhibition *The 100 Embroideries Project.* Like the name implies, the goal of the project was to create 100 embroideries, all around the same size (approximately 10 cm in diameter). | Meredith doing fieldwork. Collecting plant specimens from Awakabal Reserve, Newcastle, Australia. | Dissolving an embroidery in a bowl of warm water. | Some sculpted embroideries based on corallimorphs (mushroom coral)

Meredith Woolnough is a visual artist from the coastal town of Newcastle, Australia. Her sculptural embroideries capture the power, beauty, and fragility of nature in knotted threads. She is a graduate of the University of New South Wales with a bachelor of fine arts, has a master's in teaching from the University of Sydney, and has a BA in natural history from the University of Newcastle. She exhibits her artwork locally and internationally, and her work resides both in public and private collections worldwide. Meredith is also the author of the book *Organic Embroidery* (Schiffer Books, 2018).

Getting outside does not have to mean scuba diving or a trip to a national park. "I often do an entire project within a block of my house. I go outside and find something interesting to focus on." Meredith emphasizes that you may initially be dissatisfied with your drawing, and that is okay. There are no bad drawings. "Drawing is a learned skill, like anything else. I went back and did an entire degree because it is a learned skill, and we are all on a continuum. The only way to get better is to get started."

Meredith emphasizes, "Go out once a day or once a week. Pick a leaf and sit down and draw it for ten minutes. Sometimes it doesn't have to look like a leaf; it just has to feel like a leaf. This is the beginning of understanding."

Alice Fox
NATURE'S ALCHEMY

The time spent in the processing of natural materials, the detail of every millimeter of fiber that passes through your fingers, is expanding your understanding because of deciding to take notice. I want to convey that preciousness.

—*Alice Fox*

Nettle, bindweed, bramble, and garlic fibers drying in the allotment shed. *Photo: Alice Fox*

Alice Fox has found the secret to joy, and for her it lies in Shipley, England, a small market town in northern England.

On most days, you will find Alice working in her local garden allotment or creating in her studio. Alice approaches her allotment—and her life—with a heightened awareness of place, and the unique experience of each landscape she experiences. It is made up of fruit trees, a garden, and some random plantings that are simply volunteers in the space she was given. When she initially took over the allotment, she approached it the way Sherlock Holmes would when taking on a new case: she watched, investigated, observed. Like a foster parent, Alice adopted the life of the allotment, as it has been passed from gardener to gardener, each one leaving his or her own mark.

Not only did she inherit the growing systems but also a series of sheds and structures, replete with forgotten contents that provide a home for the treasures that Alice delights in exploring and collecting. Certainly, when most people take over an allotment, their starting point is to clear away the weeds, brush, and overgrowth that has taken over. Not Alice. For the most part, she left everything in place and began experimenting with all that she was given, processing components of the landscape in various ways to find out more about their properties and exploring what they can and cannot do.

Plot 105 is (quite literally) the seedbed for her latest adventure. "The plot is providing food for the table, so I guess it's about appreciating what is there and using it in different ways. Some of the plants [that] I don't use for fiber, I can use for dye colors or printing." Alice approaches nature with an eye for potential. Nothing is dismissed or overlooked simply because it has not been used before.

One of her initial *Plot 105* projects has been to process plants into yarn, and she has done that with other landscapes through the years. "The ball of yarn can be the most beautiful thing in itself." Alice completed an MA in creative practice at Leeds University. As part of her final thesis, she created a series of sample fibers. "To me, the series of cordage samples was simple and beautiful, and a lot of people said, 'What are you going to do with them?' I have heard that so many times. I want to help turn people's attention to what is there and what has been done to get there."

Alice's reverence for materials and process drives the work she creates. As a matter of fact, she prioritizes the process and experience of working with natural materials above the finished work and invites us to do the same. The technical constraints of each material push her to be more creative. "I'm curious about what I might find and how I might use it, whether it's a bunch of twigs or things I have found in the shed at my allotment. I get caught up in discovering the possibilities. It is so satisfying, as well as frustrating and disappointing at times. There are always these kinds of challenges with this way of working, but that is part of the journey."

While Alice's current work is focused on *Plot 105*, her creative life has always been based on a process-led practice, focused on her fascination with the landscape. For most artists, the finished piece is the center of attention. At times, artists may even keep their process to themselves until they are ready to reveal their creation or even a full exhibition of works. In contrast, Alice considers the entire undertaking as part of her work,

The world is full of obvious things which nobody by any chance ever observes.

—*Sherlock Holmes in* The Hound of the Baskervilles *by Sir Arthur Conan Doyle*

Cordage samples using plant fibers gathered from Plot 105.
Photo: Electric Egg

"Each material poses a new set of technical challenges. By working with similar materials in sequence, there is an accumulation of experience, which means that informed judgments can be made about how to work with each fiber—which ones are worth carrying on with and which are not. Alongside the physical actions of making, there is an influence of the wider personal experiences of the location where it was made: sensory stimulation, reflection, and personal experience all become tied up in the making process, so that the material is somehow imbued with those aspects.

Plot 105. *Photo: Ane Fox*

Above: Cordage made from (*clockwise from top right*) sweet-corn husk, leek, daffodil leaf, dandelion stem, nettle, bramble fiber. All gathered from Alice's allotment: Plot 105. *Photo: Alice Fox*

Left: Cordage and spun-fiber samples with looped, twined, braided, and woven structures in a variety of plant materials and found objects. *Photo: Electric Egg*

from foraging to harvesting, processing, and ultimately a resulting object or series of objects, which could take many forms. Her work includes everything from a ball of twine and collections of found items to sketches, photographs, and nutshells that have been adorned with knotting, crochet, or assemblage.

Essentially, the depth of Alice's work is found in the entire process. She relishes her way of living with her surroundings, always looking out for interesting and often-unknown materials. Her curiosity drives what she forages for and how she processes the materials, always exploring new ways to work with them. Alice savors the scent, the feel, and the various properties of each one. "I suppose I am not making a product to consume in some way. If people feel they want to own my pieces, that's great but it's not the focus."

Alice's *Plot 105* project is the latest in several undertakings that have spanned her creative life. In her *Findings* series, she collected items and thoughtfully considered them. She then created and re-created the collections, based on her experiences and thoughts related to the items, each collection forming a physical record of the place the items were gathered from.

"Collecting small items of interest is something I've done all my life. These treasures formed part of my way to understand and study the natural world around me. I see such objects that find their way into my pockets as tangible links to the places I visit."

The collections Alice assembles (and sometimes reassembles) then become the base ingredients for her manipulations and experiments. She "mends" some objects and adds on to others. She also uses these things as source material for drawings and photography. The inherent value of each piece increases as she engages with it, experiments, and adopts it as another one of the treasures in her various collections. They become imbued with her experience of the place.

Processing Flax

Growing and processing flax involves sowing seed, nurturing, weeding, harvesting, drying, rippling, retting, breaking, scutching, hackling, combing, and finally spinning. All these different processes are used to remove the fiber from the plant and reach a point where the fiber is usable for textile work.

"Each stage is enjoyable. I wouldn't go through all of that if I wasn't prepared to relish the process. At the end, the fiber has so much value for me personally, being in the place where it was grown, among the birdsong; everything else that gives me a relationship with that place imbues the materials."

"Such collections become a personal source of interest and wonder long after they are made. They form a starting point for imaginative exploration, further study, and visual representation through photography and drawing. By engaging, manipulating, and experimenting, I follow a line of inquiry. It is here that I learn about specific properties, boundaries, and possibilities. And so begins a collaboration between object and artist."

After savoring this early stage, she either pauses and assesses what she has made or pushes on, creating artwork from the materials. The art could be in the form of books, weavings, found-object assemblage, knot tying, looping, rust dyeing, creating pigments and dyes, mark making on paper, natural dyeing on fabric, photography, sketches, installations, bookmaking, and more.

"I tend to be quite experimental, much more than some people. I'm not aiming for a specific outcome. I'm happy to go with a process and see what comes out of it. It is a different kind of mindset than many artists. Because I'm using more and more of the plant material that is available, I'm exploring techniques that are new to me, learning all the time."

While *Plot 105* provides a means for understanding how Alice lives and works, how she moves through the world, it represents only her current project, and she has had many more throughout the years.

Left: Leaves and stems hand-stitched together using plant-dyed silk/cotton thread. Part of
Leaf Stitching series. *Photo: Alice Fox*

Seed case from horse chestnut, *Aesculus hippocastanum*, with needle weaving in plant-dyed
silk/cotton thread. Part of Findings series. *Photo: Alice Fox*

Seed cases from horse chestnut, *Aesculus hippocastanum*, with needle weaving and darned acorns. Part of Findings series. *Photo: Carolyn Mendelsohn*

Right: Limpet shell, *Patella vulgate*, with hand-stitched needle weaving in silk/cotton thread. Part of Findings series. *Photo: Carolyn Mendelsohn*

One of her ongoing practices is leaf stitching. She gathers leaves that are in many states, from early growth to decay, and stitches them in different ways by mending or patching them, binding them into books, or stitching them together in layers. The leaves are stitched while still fresh, and Alice creates a photographic record as they change form and decay.

Her *Tide Marks* project is a reflection on places where water meets land, always a dynamic and active environment punctuated by the clash between the land and the waves that roll in to meet it. Driven by the tidal cycles, beaches and their surroundings offer a wealth of discovery.

"What I find and work with often carries an identity and history we can only guess at. An object comes my way with the tide, with the mystery of the movement of wind, sea, and sand, or simply the consequence of human negligence."

Rust dyeing and natural dyeing are also part of Alice's body of work and have resulted in art quilts, works on paper, and artist books. Using natural dyes can be quite experimental. Much of her dyeing work includes marks and prints made using found objects from her surroundings.

Alice also began creating cordage during a family holiday. "I started by going on short walks with the young family while on holiday. I started to pick up a handful of grass and work on it. Throughout the holiday, I made a ball of string. That ball has become a record of everything I experienced during that time together." Alice recommends that we live our lives through our physical experience.

Regardless of the project, material, or processes she explores in a given landscape, Alice experiences creativity in nature unbound by outcomes. She has mastered the rich experience of engaging with the landscape in myriad ways. Walking through the world with this kind of awareness is like putting on enchanted glasses that at once allow you to see the world in new, previously unseen colors and hues.

There is no edge defining Alice's life from her work; they are one and the same. Her way of being acknowledges the temporal, and she has found that the most effective way to share it with others is to produce and share a series of self-published books that provide lasting physical evidence of a full project. Her books serve as a conduit to communicate her entire experience to us. She invites us to join her in actively experiencing nature, fostering an enduring sense of thoughtful curiosity, methodical experimentation and processing of the materials, and engagement with it in a variety of ways.

"The time spent in the process with natural materials, the detail of every millimeter of fiber that passes through your fingers, helps your understanding expand because you are noticing things. I want to convey that preciousness."

Go Outside

We can all find a path to the rich experiences that Alice engages in, every day. Embark on your own today by giving her trial-and-error method a try. In Alice's words, "One of the things I always say to people is that you don't really know what a material is like to work with until you have had a go. You must do it yourself. The best way is to just do it. Gather materials, try to manipulate them, learn what you can do with them. The materials you find will drive what you can do. Relish that process. Gather something today. It could be as simple as a handful of twigs. Bring them inside, bundle them with other fibers or found items." Consider other ways of engaging with the materials you find. Sketch them or create collections. You will be on your way to actively engaging with your environment in much the same way as Alice does.

Left to Right: "Rippling" flax to remove seed heads from dried stems before retting. *Photo: Alice Fox* | Leaves hand-stitched together to form small "patch-work," using plant-dyed silk/cotton thread. Part of Leaf Stitching series. *Photo: Alice Fox* | *Photo: Carolyn Mendelsohn* | Limpet shell, *Patella vulgate*, with hand-stitched needle weaving in silk/cotton thread. Part of Findings series. *Photo: Alice Fox*

Alice Fox's process-led practice is based on personal engagement with the landscape and has sustainability at its heart. She works with natural fibers and gathered materials, employing natural dyes, stitching, weaving, and soft basketry techniques in different combinations to make surfaces and structures. Meaning is embedded in the materials she chooses to use. Alice studied contemporary surface design & textiles at Bradford School of Arts & Media and completed an MA in creative practice at Leeds Arts University. She works from her studio in Saltaire, West Yorkshire, UK. She exhibits, lectures, and teaches workshops nationally and internationally.

"It's playing. That's what we're doing. Actually, play is what it is all about. When I'm starting with a new material, I'm playing." Alice recommends that we live our lives through our physical experience. "If people appreciate what I'm saying, the next time they pick things up outdoors, they are more likely to see the possibilities."

Munir Jones
CHERISHING LIFE'S TREASURES

Even if you never have the chance to see or touch the ocean, the ocean touches you with every breath you take, every drop of water you drink, every bite you consume. Everyone, everywhere is inextricably connected to and utterly dependent upon the existence of the sea.

—*Dr. Sylvia Earle, oceanographer and author of* The World Is Blue: How Our Fate and the Ocean's are One

While connection with nature has long been seen as a link to general health and well-being, it is even more important now than ever.

Time spent in nature also makes us more compassionate, reduces anxiety, and helps us open up to relating to others more meaningfully. These benefits came to mind when I connected with Munir Jones, an artist whose work is tied not only to his surroundings but also to his generous character. Munir's natural warmth has been fostered by a lifetime of unique experiences.

"I spent most of my professional career working with at-risk adolescents who were suicidal, lived in dysfunctional situations, or worse. I still have kids contacting me and asking me how I'm doing. They thank me and tell me that I saved their lives." Even several years into his official retirement, Munir misses the connection with the kids. He feels that he developed a unique way of working with them, and that it was a reflection of the solo path he has walked creating his art, along with other challenges and projects he has taken on throughout his life. "What I did with those kids was to share my own life stories, of a time when Black people like me were not allowed into many places.

"When I was five years old, my parents sent me to my grandparents' house in Tennessee to live on a farm that had no running water or gas. We also lived off what we grew. I told a lot of the kids these stories. They were really intrigued." The same generosity and compassion Munir shared with the kids comes through in the artwork he creates.

Munir's pieces begin with the gathering process on one of several beaches in Southern California and results in dimensional, woven work that integrates driftwood, moonstone, beach glass, fishing line, and other materials.

Munir is quick to mention that each of his pieces is distinctive. The nature of his work ensures that he never creates two identical pieces. One can certainly see that his art and his career have been created and lived on his terms. Munir has always lived an authentic life, taking on challenges and hobbies that were not expected of him as a Black man. His life story is evident in his creations and in the generous way he lives. "I want to share my love of the beaches and the weavings with others. Most people feel a strong connection to the places I depict right away. My weavings give them an object that takes them back to their memories of that particular beach."

Munir's inherent desire to make dimensional work along with his deep connection to the ocean are what catapulted him into his original style. For all of his professional life, he longed to be on the California beaches. Retirement provided him the opportunity to spend his days walking the beaches and letting his mind wander to his next creation. Many artists integrate driftwood here and there, but Munir utilizes it as an integral framework for his art. He scouts out and harvests large branches and tree trunks that have washed up on shore, then nests his weaving into the negative spaces provided by each piece.

Once Munir began making dimensional work that is directly connected to the California oceanside, he knew that he had found his creative path. "I have always loved the ocean. I learned how to weave in Hermosa Beach. The second weaving that I did was a response to the sun reflecting off the water. From then on, I used the ocean as my inspiration."

Throughout his life, Munir's mother has consistently

I want to help others create meaningful connections with or reinforce the nostalgia they already feel for the beaches along the Southern California coast.

—Munir Jones

Top: Munir finds greens very hard to do, but with lots of patience, this one came together. He used grape wood on this weaving.

Bottom: Munir in his old studio holding his weaving of an abstract fish

Right: Pea-sized pebbles on the beach of Moonstone Beach in Cambria, California

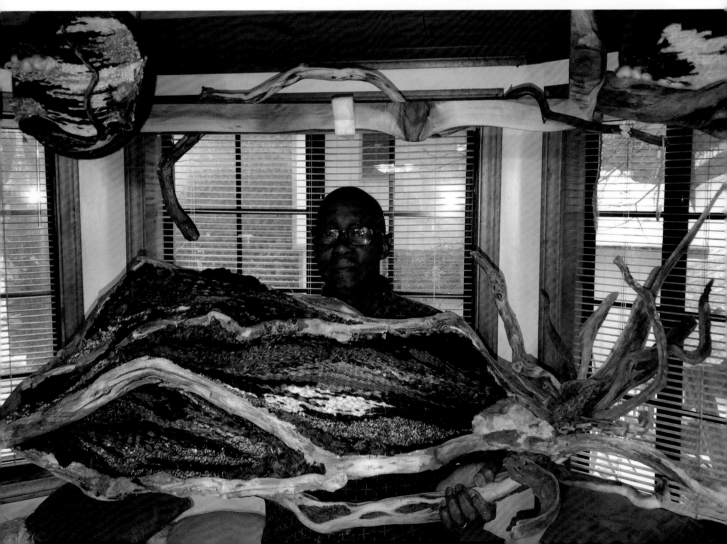

"I carry a bag of moonstones in my pocket so I can share them with people wherever I go. It is an easy way to share the magic."

encouraged and believed in him. "God gave me this talent, and my mom nurtured it. Every time there was a project in school, she would help me, and I would get the best feedback every time. So, as I went along, I would always do things that were different. People would say, 'Black people don't do this or that . . .' That's how I got to where I am. In the '70s I found a jewelry store that made only one-of-a-kind jewelry, and that left an impression. So that is what I do with my art."

For many of his pieces, the wood came from Hermosa Beach, near his home. Other materials come from different beaches in his area and include moonstone, sea glass, and more natural findings. "People seem to really love the ocean. They may request a piece with particular materials from their favorite beaches. I want to help others create meaningful connections with or reinforce the nostalgia they already feel for the beaches along the Southern California coast." Each piece Munir creates is marked with the name of the beach and the date he found the materials.

Each item that Munir collects is imbued with the energy of the place by which it is inspired. He said, "I tell people, if a piece of wood or rock doesn't talk to me, it stays on the beach." For the last several years, Munir has brought a friend along on many of his gathering trips. Munir frequently breaks the news that they will not be using some of the materials that his friend gathered, because they just don't speak to him. For Munir, the creative process relies on his conversations with each found component.

Until recently, Munir's studio was located in an extra room of his house. He has outgrown that space and moved his work into a shed in his yard. Now he is heartened to have a dedicated space for his art, which is opening even more pathways to his creativity and mission of connecting people to the sanctuary offered by special places in nature.

"I was using a room in my house, but I blew it out. I couldn't work there anymore. My wife told me to order a shed, so now I have an art studio in my yard. It's still not a very large space, but for me, with what I have, it works well. I have all my tools, a great selection of driftwood, all my fibers, and I'm ready to go. I just finished the shed recently, so I'm ready to bust loose!"

For Munir's weaving, he uses a variety of fibers that evoke the textures of the beaches that inspired them. This means using commercial wool, mottled fibers, and sometimes his own hand-dyed wool, dyed precisely to achieve the nuanced colors of the ocean.

People tend to have a visceral, emotional response to Munir's work. He attributes that to the divine inspiration that led him along this path. "God gave me this talent to create and to produce and give people something different that nobody else does." Munir's embrace of the divine and commitment to living with compassion work together to make magic.

This was a special-order piece, the biggest Munir has ever done, 43 inches in size. The new owner was very happy to see her new piece.

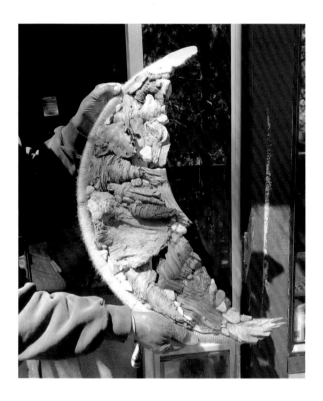

Left: One of Munir's crescent moons includes moonstones, driftwood, sea glass, beach stones, and pinewood knots.

Bottom: Sitting sculpture, using driftwood found on Moonstone Beach in Cambria, California

Go Outside

Munir's advice is to let your mind be open and free when you are in nature. "That is how I came to be how I am. For me, my advice would be to let your mind's eye wander. I can look at a piece of wood or a rock and see that I can make something of it. It's all about the creative force."

People often perceive or interpret things in Munir's art that he doesn't see. It reminds him that everybody brings something different to their viewpoint and how they experience their surroundings. He also believes that you can be creative in many ways that are often unexpected. Take every opportunity to spend time outside, foster creativity in your own way, and enjoy the increased sense of well-being and generosity.

Munir Jones creates three-dimensional woven pieces that include driftwood and other materials. He also makes abstract pen-and-ink drawings. Munir began weaving in 1978 after several years as a jewelry maker. His work is divinely inspired, and each piece is intended to personally connect the viewer with the place where it began. He lives and works in Lake Arrowhead, California.

Left to right: Chenille given to Munir by friends | Munir Jones holding his very large weaving with a beautiful piece of manzanita | Windy shores, driftwood from Moonstone Beach in Cambria, California | Another loom in its beginning.

Nicole Dextras
EMBRACING IMPERMANENCE

The environment, after all, is where we all meet, where we all have a mutual interest. It is one thing that all of us share. It is not only a mirror of ourselves, but a focusing lens on what we can become.

—*Lady Bird Johnson,*
first lady of the United States (1963–69),
speech at Yale University,
White House diary, October 9, 1967

Bouquet: outdoor sculpture of frozen fabric done at the Banff Centre for the Arts. Melted quickly.

With ease and warmth, Nicole Dextras led me through the magical, eco-fiction world that she has created.

She aspires to replace the polarized conversation that typically frames environmental issues with an invitation to awaken our own curiosity and foster our inherent resourcefulness. "I want to tell a story from another point of view—the idea that our resourcefulness is an antidote to the fear and violence that is most often paired with the trope about environmental disasters." She gently, creatively shepherds us into her magical world, teaching us to explore our own ingenuity in the environment. Nicole combines her background in theater and a lifelong interest in the environment to create installations and costumes that have expanded into filmmaking.

Nicole has an acute awareness of the ephemeral. She brings our attention to the fleeting nature of the world around us and is committed to making work that is temporary and naturally decomposes.

"It goes against everything we have been taught about getting work into museums, getting work seen and collected." She is often given unsolicited advice about the chemical treatments she might use to preserve her work. That, of course, shows a fundamental misunderstanding of her plea to us to celebrate the impermanence of nature itself. Still, those comments give her the opportunity to start positive conversations about the meaning imbued in her work.

The initial concept behind Nicole's creative path planted itself in her mind when she discovered ice as a creative medium. It was winter, and she started to build installations that were fundamentally temporary by virtue of their connection with the season. She said, "The freezing and melting process with the ice installations provided the spark behind the idea. I wanted to make a parallel with nature. It is ephemeral and so are we. This led to my work following the seasons, following the patterns of nature." With the arrival of spring, Nicole started to explore costumes created exclusively from natural materials, and the path forward revealed itself to her.

Instead of using fabric and other traditional costuming materials, she utilizes leaves, flowers, and other foraged materials. Instead of a needle and thread, she often uses thorns to sew leaves together. But Nicole does so much more than simply build magical, organic costumes. Through her work, she coaxes us toward the realization that we are an integral part of the natural environment; it is not separate from us. The performative aspect of many of her pieces also means that viewers engage with and actually *become* part of the work.

"We used to think that telling people the facts about environmental issues would instigate change, but it didn't. Instead, it overwhelmed the public and made us more jaded. So, it got me thinking more deeply into the reasons behind why that wasn't working. And part of the reason is that we are disconnected from nature. Our entire idea of nature is that it is a resource. We don't see ourselves as part of the ecosystem."

Although these days it is more common to come across costumes that are seemingly made from natural materials, they are typically not. Many are created with commercial cut (or even plastic) flowers, glue guns, staples, and other crutches to creation used to attract attention in shop windows. Nicole's commitment to exclusively utilizing natural materials makes her work unique. The resulting

114

Ideas come to me
when I am in the
forest. When you
relax yourself, it's as if
the creative things are
already there; they
just have the chance
to emerge.
—Nicole Dextras

"I wanted to try working with natural materials, and while I observed land art that was being made, I didn't see myself in that area and didn't see myself fitting into that scene. I wanted to create something original. So connecting garments to the environment felt unique and like a more personal way for me to talk about the ephemeral aspects of nature."

costumes represent the beginning of a process of change that is integral to the work.

Nicole has built characters and spun backstories for each piece she creates. "The narratives built themselves. It happened on its own. It came naturally to me, and it happened without me knowing it. It wasn't integral to anything other than how I could connect with the model or character. The power of the stories lies in their ability to help us make that fundamental connection with nature." The backstories offered a way to describe the hypothetical character wearing the costumes to the models who were displaying them. As she worked in her studio, her mind was at work imagining the eco-fictional reality that each character lives in. Over time, the narratives expanded into alternative worlds. You could say that they took on a life of their own. These background narratives led to the engaging, performative projects that Nicole is known for.

Typically, the public is a partner in Nicole's work. They are observers as she searches for locations, forages for materials, and builds sets and costumes, and ultimately when she sends her characters out into the world to interact with the community. She considers herself an urban forager. She often harvests her materials from public spaces. The act of gathering materials itself is when the engagement begins, as curious bystanders ask about her work.

The characters she has built started with her *WEEDrobes* series. Nicole placed the characters into unique, existing environments that she scouted out and identified as embodying the essence of each one.

Viewers continue to be active participants in her environmental performances when they engage with completed pieces. These characters bring their performances and messages to the public in a live theater of learning that takes place on city streets, in parks, and in other settings.

As Nicole shared the story of her work with me, it seemed that the progression to on-site, performative art was inevitable. Her characters were able to fully embody their backstory and deepen their impact by mingling with the public. For example, with the piece titled *Laurel Suffragette*, Miss Laurel Green-Fairfashion brings awareness to the historical significance and current state of the textile industrial complex.

Over the years, Nicole has spent time on the streets of Montreal, Canada, and in the garment district of New York City, among other places, doing street interventions and engaging communities in real time. The photographs and videos of those live installations continue the conversations that were started in the live settings.

The *WEEDrobes* series eventually expanded into the Botanical Wearables collections, where Nicole developed other concepts such as the *Little Green Dress Project*. That gave her the opportunity to further develop her skills for creating costumes entirely from compostable materials and explore other topics, such as consumerism, feminism, and awareness of the environment.

These cultivated stories guide us through the ideas she invites us to explore. "I want to help people consider the environment and our role as part of it, not separate from it. In this way the costumes are quite literally breaking

Laurel Suffragette is a time traveler who had witnessed the 1911 Triangle Shirtwaist Factory disaster, which caused the deaths of garment workers in NYC. A century later, she appears on the streets of an urban fashion district to gauge the pulse of today's attitudes about the fashion industry.

"Wear It and Compost It" is the tagline for the Weedrobes series. Nicole's garments are often left in her garden after a performance, where she continues to document the process of their return back to nature.

"People often try to give me ideas of how I could preserve my work. But the point is that it is going to decay, and it will still be beautiful when it decays. Being an environmental artist isn't just about working with natural materials. It is about learning that I am part of nature, not separate from nature. I am working with things that are ephemeral, that aren't going to last. It's teaching me how to let go."

This page: Versailles Nature / Elle (Wedding with Nature): Eco-wedding dress exemplifying our symbiotic relationship with nature. Paris, 2020.

Left page clockwise from top left: Barbara: magnolia leaves, hydrangea flowers, globe thistle, and thorns | Ferns, moss, thistles, magnolia seed pod, vines

Above: The Mobile Garden Dress engages with the public about plants and sustainability.

Photo: E. Stoner

Right: By asking children to touch the plant's soil and then water it, Lena helps them understand the basic premise of environmental stewardship: we need to work with nature.

down the division between us and our environment."

One such example is her *Mobile Garden Dress*, whose character Madame Jardin mingles with the public, talking with them about the environment. She even encourages people to water her garden and try some of the vegetables, herbs, and greens that she is growing on her dress. The dress also acts as a tent; she literally carries her home and food with her. The garment not only is fully compostable but is able to sustain her life. This piece is an astute example of Nicole's vision for us being brought into a reality that we can experience firsthand.

Because the backstories were already forming in her mind, it was a small leap from photographing the pieces to making films about them. She was already creating sets for the characters to be photographed in; filming them has allowed her to more widely share the work. "Photography and filmmaking make you see." She is currently creating a series of short films. Each one explores a different concept related to the environment.

The first film in the series, *Waiting for Spring; Persephone and the Pomegranate*, features a character dressed in a jacket made from pomegranate peels. It tells the story of a future, eco-fictional woman who relies on the healing benefits of pomegranates to reintegrate into a world that has experienced a collapse of the food economy as a result of forest fires.

"I set my work in the future as an alternative to the reductive postapocalyptic fictions depicted in Hollywood films. My scenarios envision the determination to rebuild, and they embody the resilience and empathy repeatedly demonstrated in numerous tragedies. Therefore, the survivors in this new world are not the scantily clad, heavily armed warriors portrayed in video games. They are more akin to the makers and hackers who already exist at the margins of society today."

Viewers of the films and participants in Nicole's live learning installations are scooped up and wrapped in the otherworldly reality that Nicole has created for us. "I want to show characters who are in their own precarious environment but are surviving because of their creativity and a natural desire to live, as well as their creative-thinking abilities." Nicole integrates us into her world; it is a world where we recognize our fundamental connection with nature and are invited to participate.

Persephone's jacket is made from pomegranate peels attached with thorns.

Created for the *Earth Art* exhibition at VanDusen Botanical Garden, the Little Green Dress Projekt consisted of twenty-one dresses made entirely with plant materials over a period of two months.

The Mobile Garden Dress is a self-sustaining garden and flexible shelter for the new urban nomad, complete with pots of edible plants and a hoop skirt, which converts into a tent at night.

Go Outside

Time spent in nature builds a sense of context for our lives.

Consider your own narrative about the world you live in, and the part you play in it. Reframe the story of how you consider environmental issues, as part of your own life. This can spread from your place in the environment to your place in the world and the roles you play within them. Have confidence in your own resourcefulness as it relates to the environment around you and the challenges you are facing. Time in nature will help you build that resiliency and acceptance of the temporal, both in your physical surroundings and the ups and downs of life.

"A useful exercise is to make some kind of land art. Make a pattern with leaves. Choose your materials. Through that process you need to figure out that it's not going to last. It's a certain acknowledgment of the real process of nature. It is not just a cute picture that gets likes on social media. Focus on creating your own authentic experience in nature."

Nicole Dextras is an award-winning environmental artist working in a multitude of media, having created art installations in Spain, Mongolia, and Canada and throughout the US. She is a graduate of the Emily Carr University of Art in Vancouver, British Columbia, Canada. Nicole describes her work as a radical form of organic self-expression, with environmental issues at the core. She shows us how to experience our surroundings in a unique way and explore our own resourcefulness to address the environment and our own creative path.

Left to right: Gathering materials for a project | By asking children to touch the plant's soil and then water it, Lena helps them understand the basic premise of environmental stewardship: we need to work with nature. | Harvesting fireweed at a community garden | Ferns, moss, thistles, magnolia seed pod, vines

Maleah Bretz
DRAWING CLOSER

I think I could do this forever. I am honored when someone entrusts me to create a piece for them based on their most cherished and profound experiences. It is amazing to help them revisit those moments of their lives.

—*Maleah Bretz*

Isle of Skye, Scotland, 2020, various fibers and driftwood

Maleah Bretz's woven works began as a direct representation of places and experiences from her own life.

Before she knew it, she was making these powerful pieces to help others revisit and celebrate watershed moments in their lives. While Maleah was working through her studio art major at the University of North Carolina at Asheville, her life was buoyed by nature.

She spent every free moment hiking in the Blue Ridge Mountains, discovering hidden waterfalls and old-growth forests and taking in the layers of mountains, each with a deeper haze hovering over them. These experiences happened during the same period of her life when she was synthesizing her identity as an artist. Nature and art became one.

Although her degree originally focused on sculpture, she gradually integrated weaving. Her first foray into sculptural weaving was a set of five weavings—although Maleah points out that calling them "sculptural" was a stretch. What they did was help her make the transition to working in fibers.

Within a two-year block, Maleah had lived in five homes, stretching from the Philippines to Chicago to Asheville. "They were five 'homes' that I had in those two years." Each component of her initial weaving series focused on one of those homes. Although the seed of an idea was planted with that series, Maleah feels that the works lacked depth of story. At the time she felt transient and lacking the fundamental feelings and emotional connections of a true *home*. "The project was a way to try to come to terms with finding peace in having several homes. They were at once all and none of them my home."

A move to Chicago in 2019 swept her into an entirely different life, where her artistic identity hibernated while she worked in the unrelated field of social work. While still in Chicago, it was difficult to fully embrace nature. So she did what she could to bring little bits of art back into her world. She pulled out some of her fibers and weaving frames and started working at home. "Even dabbling just a bit in the creative realm was so peaceful for me." However, what her life was still missing was the nature-and-art blend that had fed her creative spirit back in North Carolina.

The structure Maleah had built for her life in the city was shaken loose by becoming pregnant with her first child, resulting in a dramatic reassessment of priorities. That is when Maleah found her way back "home" to art.

Maleah's move back to the Smoky Mountain region in 2020 had a welcome impact on her life. She dove into her studio practice as soon as she landed back in the nature-infused environment. She started creating pieces that weren't exact reproductions or reflections of nature but were subtly inspired by a photo of nature. "They were from my childhood or other places that I had strong memories of; they offered those clear memories such as childhood beach trips." She made several pieces in the collection of weavings that intentionally rekindled strong experiences for her. While they were not directly based on photos, they represented the first step along the way.

"The backstory that I included with completed pieces inspired people. As a result, they started to send me photographs that held special memories for them, and asked if I would do the same for them. Some photographs represented faraway hometowns, some represented meaningful family trips to Ireland and Lake Powell,

Many eyes go through the meadow, but few see the flowers in it.
—*Ralph Waldo Emerson*

Mt. Diablo, 2020, various fibers and wooden dowel

Asheville, 2020, various fibers and wooden dowel. This piece was commissioned by an Asheville native, but Maleah found it fun to work on, since Asheville holds such a special place in her heart!

133

Utah, while others held truly deep memories such as a last family vacation before a brother was diagnosed and began his battle with cancer. That was the most beautiful thing to me, to be invited into this special love and special moment for this family." Maleah considers being asked into that personal, intimate space an honor. She holds those pieces in reverence while she works on them, meditating on the feelings and life experiences that she wants to acknowledge and help them cherish.

In the past year, Maleah's unique woven works have taken off in a way that she had never imagined. Although they represent a scene in nature, the term "landscape" does not do justice to the impact her works create in the lives of the people she makes them for. Although Maleah has always used photos from her own life as a base for her work, recently she has also used the experiences of others.

"I think I could do this forever. When someone has a special memory and it is important to them, for whatever reason, to create a piece for them that takes them back to that moment is amazing." Whether it's a commission piece or her own work, Maleah's weavings frame and explore life experiences in a new way, intensifying the memories.

With each commission, she asks the recipient to share the backstory behind the scene depicted in the photo. Leah carries that heartfelt narrative and those emotions into

the piece while working on it. That process brings her pure joy. She is assisting people by helping them recover (and sometimes heal from) events, emotions, and relationships that they may have lost. The works represent a portal in time to that memory and the feelings of that moment.

With regard to Maleah's actual process, she focuses on color first, then enlists texture to broaden the work and accomplish the effects she seeks. But the heavy lifting is done with color. For the most part, she utilizes a repeated Arya knot and uses recycled, secondhand, repurposed, and commercial raw fibers, which she dyes herself. "When I dye them myself, I can create nuanced colors and emulate nature's gradients." Maleah accomplishes delicate hues by waiting in between each dye bath, letting the vat fade before she dips again. "With each piece, I can use up to fifty types of fibers. I love finding cast-off yarn collections at Goodwill and other places, so I can get in touch with the subtlety of the image."

Maleah's husband is a musician and worship leader at their local church. Together they are fostering a lifestyle that embraces nature, music, and art at its core. "We both would rather use the gifts that we have been given to give something back than to use them just for ourselves. For me, personally, getting to meditate on who God is, through this beautiful landscape, draws me closer to God's heart as his child."

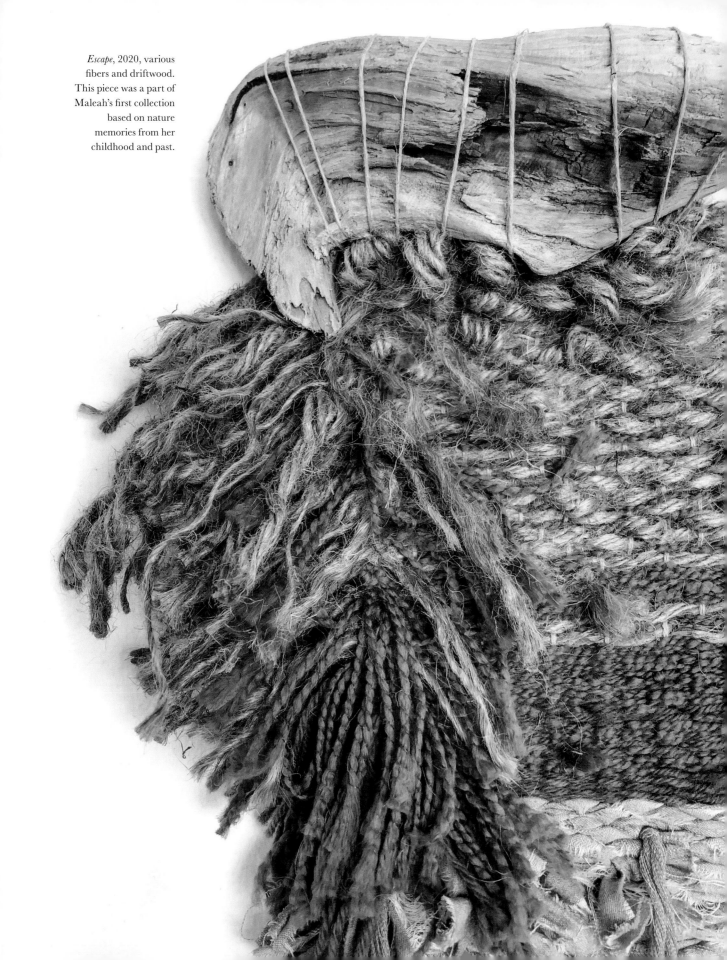

Escape, 2020, various fibers and driftwood. This piece was a part of Maleah's first collection based on nature memories from her childhood and past.

Sedona, 2020, various fibers and driftwood. This piece was special to Maleah, since it was commissioned only a few months after she had visited Sedona, Arizona, with her family. She found the feel of this landscape fresh and exciting.

Go Outside

For Maleah, art and nature give her the exceptional opportunity to experience the divine. The rich, nature-inspired, spiritual experiences she creates for herself are also spread to others through her art. Maleah is secure in her enduring faith that you can experience the divine through a combination of creativity and nature to awaken your imagination, find refuge, and foster spirituality in your life.

Left to right: Pictured are some of the hand-dyed fibers Maleah likes to incorporate into weaving to achieve a gradient affect, which is so often and beautifully found in nature. | *Banff National Park*, 2020, various fibers and wooden dowel. This piece was commissioned for a newly married couple. This photograph was taken as they were getting engaged. | The morning sun rising over the Blue Ridge Mountains at one of Maleah's favorite spots along the parkway, the Pisgah Inn | Maleah weaving with her daughter, 2021.

Maleah Bretz is a North Carolina fiber artist whose primary inspiration is derived from nature and memories created within nature. She uses landscape photographs provided by her clients to create meaningful, one-of-a-kind pieces of woven wall art. Her hope is to create works of art that are portals back in time to a beautiful memory.

"You could use any medium to do what I do. Paint, draw, sculpt, anything. The most important thing is to allow yourself time and space to rest in a memory. In our culture we are so obsessed with what comes next. In the past, people would talk about memories and stories and allow themselves to rest there, in that time and place. Give yourself an hour—or at least thirty minutes. Actually print out a photograph, don't just view one on a screen, and think about what it means for you. Recapture the moment of that memory, including the look, feel, scents, and more. See what flows from that."

Lorraine Roy
LAYERS OF UNDERSTANDING

When Mother Trees—the majestic hubs at the center of forest communication, protection, and sentience—die, they pass their wisdom to their kin, generation after generation, sharing the knowledge of what helps and what harms, who is friend or foe, and how to adapt and survive in an ever-changing landscape. It's what all parents do.

—Suzanne Simard, PhD

This Avian Heart #2 (Blue Jay), 2019, 35-inch wall hanging. Blue jays have a mutually beneficial relationship with red oaks. The trees supply them with nesting sites, soft insects for their young, and acorns to store for the winter. Blue jays help propagate the oaks by burying the acorns for later and forgetting where they put them!

Most days, Lorraine Roy can be found in her studio and gallery, a freestanding building surrounded by thriving natural and herb gardens on her property at the top of the Niagara Escarpment near the western edge of Lake Ontario.

The Niagara Escarpment, the long cliff that was formed as a result of faulting or erosion, is located in the United States and Canada and runs predominantly east–west from New York through Ontario, Michigan, Wisconsin, and Illinois. It is most famous as the cliff over which the Niagara River plunges at Niagara Falls, for which it is named. Although Lorraine's work includes explorations of bees and other small creatures, her overarching lifelong work is concentrated on portraying trees and their related systems, the foundation of which lies in her scientific background.

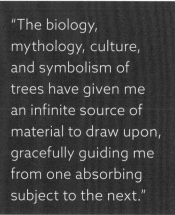

"The biology, mythology, culture, and symbolism of trees have given me an infinite source of material to draw upon, gracefully guiding me from one absorbing subject to the next."

She started there and has spent thirty years uncovering the riveting stories of nature's interconnected systems—the complex networks that work collaboratively, unbeknown to the rest of us, who tend to notice only the "drive by" versions of the trees in our midst. For Lorraine, each bit of knowledge that she has gained over the years has added a new level of understanding, much like the rings of a tree.

"I always go back to the natural sciences for fresh inspiration, as they provide endless possibilities. I keep an eye on breaking botanical research. New findings can set off a whole fresh set of imagery for a series. I often contact the researchers to see if they are interested in answering specific questions and sharing information. This adds depth to my work and provides facts I can share with the audiences for my talks.

"Nothing has influenced me more than my degree in horticulture. This background in the natural sciences gave me the basics for my own searches for information, and a way to approach and understand scientists in the fields I want to focus on."

Lorraine's curiosity about trees and their rings led to the development of her recent series, titled *Woven Wood*. This series has been so relatable, as interest in nature and environmentalism increases, that it spent three years being exhibited across Canada. *Woven Wood* began with a raft of questions about tree rings. "Tree rings are a living journal of a tree's history: its growth, development, and endurance. They record events in the life of a tree by building layer upon layer of fresh cells, leaving the marks of events forever preserved within. I was intrigued. My new task was to explore a question: What can tree rings teach me?"

Armed with her scientific background and a healthy curiosity, in 2017, Lorraine set out to find an expert who could help inform her series. As fate would have it, she found Dr. Suzanne Simard, a researcher and professor at the University of British Columbia, Lorraine's alma mater. As a dendrochronologist, Dr. Simard studies tree rings to learn about the relationship between climate and tree growth, in an effort to reconstruct past climates.

My thoughts take a quiet stroll through the day's creative journey, where my eyes and hands lead me outward from the warm heart of a tree, and back in again.

—Lorraine Roy

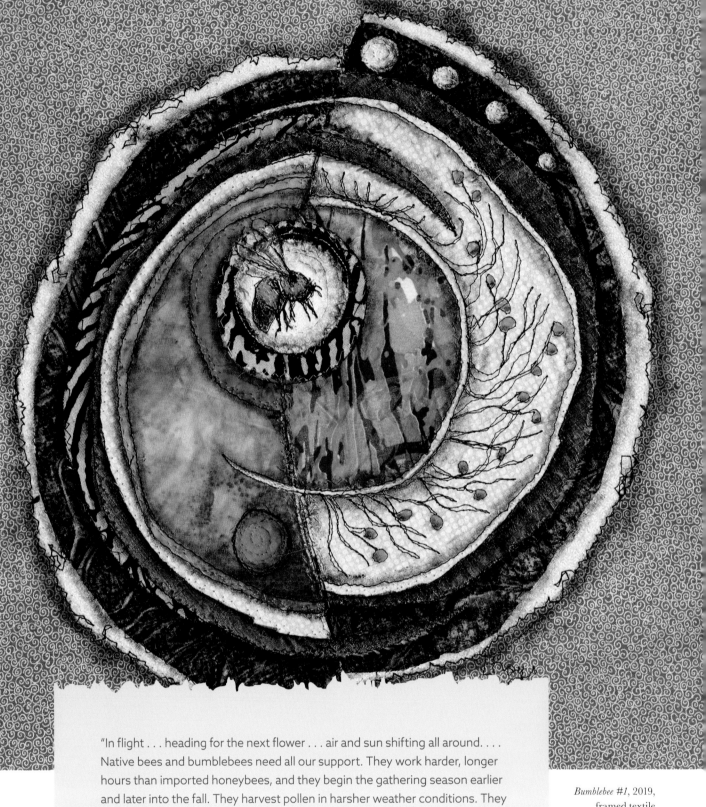

"In flight . . . heading for the next flower . . . air and sun shifting all around. . . . Native bees and bumblebees need all our support. They work harder, longer hours than imported honeybees, and they begin the gathering season earlier and later into the fall. They harvest pollen in harsher weather conditions. They are also important pollinators for the more challenging legume flowers such as alfalfa. Over four hundred species of native bees call Ontario their home. On my property in Dundas, I have been planting more native shrubs and flowers and stopped using all chemicals and fertilizers. Watching them work the flowers has become my favorite summer pastime!"

Bumblebee #1, 2019, framed textile

"I wanted to know what it would be like to re-create, with sewing thread, the tree rings of a one-hundred-year-old tree. With my tree rings pieces, I examine how trees faithfully hold their stories within them, just as they commit to staying planted in one place for their entire lives. This was a long project—sewing that many rings, even with a fast machine, is a dizzying experience!"

One Hundred Years, detail of 2018 wall hanging

While this part of her work is known as dendroclimatology, Lorraine soon learned there were several more research pathways. Climate research was just the starting point. The next step was the revelation of the integral role of the fungal mat, an organism that covers the forest floor. This complex web of connections underground can be interpreted as thousands of fungal organisms or one massive, connected organism—a humongous fungus!

Fungal mats are responsible for increasing nutrient availability to trees by increasing the efficiency by which nutrients are recycled, releasing phosphorus and other plant nutrients from mineral soils and removing inorganic plant nutrients from soil solution.[1] Approximately 90 percent of all vascular land plants live in some association with mycorrhizal fungi. Mycorrhizal associations are seen in the fossil record and are believed to be one of the contributing factors that allowed early land plants, including *Aglaophyton major* (one of the first land plants), to conquer the land.[2]

Initially hesitant to reach out, Lorraine was pleased to find that Dr. Simard was an enthusiastic advocate for dendrology, giving her a full tour of the Simard Lab in the Department of Forestry at the University of Ontario at Guelph. Lorraine was captivated.

Gradually this unique alliance led to Lorraine's *Woven*

Wood exhibition, a series of twenty-three circular wall works ranging from 2 to 3 feet in diameter, each one investigating the interconnectedness below the forest floor, where a comprehensive system between fungi and tree roots provides a surprising line of communication and resource exchanges among trees. In Lorraine's words, "In the top 6 inches of the forest floor lies a vast and flourishing communication system as old as photosynthesis itself. An exquisitely balanced symbiotic relationship between mycorrhizal fungi and tree roots exists in this narrow band, providing a network of channels for resources and messages between individual trees. The resulting plant chatter is as complex and efficient as our own World Wide Web. This mycorrhizal network thus connects and stabilizes the forest and, by extension, our entire planet's biosphere."

Each piece in the series explores another complex and seemingly implausible system. For example, in the piece titled *Seeds*, Lorraine shares one of the many amazing discoveries by Dr. Simard that revealed how germinating seeds on the forest floor produce enzymes that activate the germination of fungal spores. "This is especially important where the seedlings fall onto the surfaces that do not already have a fungal mat."

In the piece titled *The Salmon Forest*, Lorraine shares

"I may be the only one who ever used the humble gypsy moth as a source of inspiration! Yet, this is one important little insect. Ever since its accidental release in 1868 by a French scientist on the East Coast of the US, this intrepid traveler has become responsible for the defoliation of millions of forest trees. In this piece I wanted to show how trees record insect depredation in their rings . . . a slower year of growth results in a much-narrower ring, and recovery can take a few years. No matter what we do now, the gypsy moth is here to stay, and we are ever more responsible to encourage its many natural predators to thrive and survive."

Gypsy Moth, 2019,
framed textile

This Avian Heart #3 (Chickadee),
2020, wall hanging

"Chickadees are a welcome visitor to the garden. They are tireless insect eaters, and when feeding a clutch of babies, they collect thousands of soft larvae. I've portrayed this one with native wild cherry, *Prunus virginiana*, a lovely small tree that hosts a broad spectrum of butterfly and moth caterpillars and produces tiny sour red fruits, both of which nourish birds. Chickadees like to nest in tree crevices with up to twelve eggs in a clutch."

one of the amazing ways that science has learned to study ancillary environments to trees by researching their rings. This piece tells the story of how a nitrogen isotope found in migrating salmon ends up in the rings of trees. "When the salmon run up the rivers to spawn, they are either captured by wildlife or die after laying their eggs. Bears drag the salmon remains back into the woods, where they decompose, becoming an important source of nitrogen for the trees. The trees hold the banks and keep the river water fresh. A special heavy nitrogen isotope, 15N, can be directly traced from the salmon to the tree rings. In testing, it is then possible to determine the relative populations of migrating salmon from year to year, for the entire life span of the tree."

For Lorraine's *Wisdom of the Rings* series, which she began in 2019, also a study in trees, she connected with Dr. Ze've Gedalof, professor at the University of Ontario, Guelph. His research addresses forest ecosystem dynamics, climatic variability, and natural-resources management at the Climate & Ecosystem Dynamics Research (CEDaR) Laboratory. Dr. Gedalof was very enthusiastic about Lorraine's work, and he also has a background in art. She visited his lab, where he showed her tree rings at a microscopic level, taught her about the coring equipment that is used to pull out samples from the center of the trees, and more. This is where Lorraine initially was introduced to such remarkable concepts as tree rings that can be as small as a couple of cells in width.

"He showed all the equipment and all the samples they have collected over the years along the escarpment. Arguably, the oldest trees in Canada are on the Niagara Escarpment. They may have trunks as narrow as a human wrist, but that's because of the slow growth. The oldest tree in the area, a white cedar, is 1,400 years old. They have biological advantages that make them able to grow on rock."

Lorraine's *Wisdom of the Rings* series resulted in an exhibition and talk that she and Dr. Gedalof presented at the university. Ironically, she ended up speaking about the science at play behind the art, and he spoke about her art that was based on science.

Lorraine is very attracted to how nature has influenced the religions we have today, and her *Spirit Trees* series reflects how some of the stories we regard in religion today include the same lessons that Native religious beliefs have embraced for hundreds of years, which are based on the cycles and wisdom of nature. In Lorraine's words, "For example, in a Christian context, the main message was for humans to love each other. Now we know that trees share resources with each other, a form of love and connection within nature. Indigenous people knew that intuitively. Now we see that it is happening in science as well. Science confirms what Indigenous populations already knew."

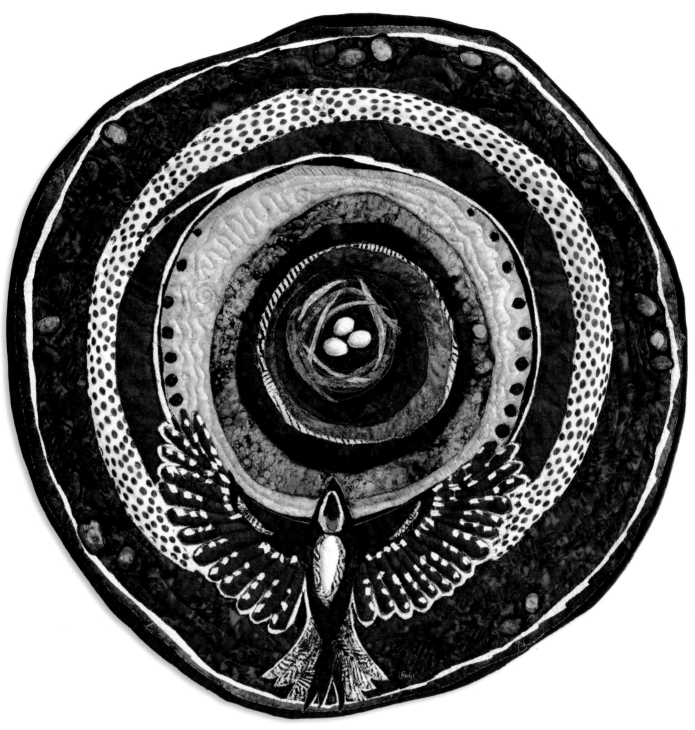

This Avian Heart #1 (Downy Woodpecker),
2019, fabric wall hanging

Tree Rings, wall hanging from Woven Woods

Lorraine gains her knowledge and follows her creative muse by working in series. She suggests staying with one theme while you really study it. "I like working in series, and some of mine have been running along for over twenty years. I keep revisiting themes with fresh ideas. I'm obsessed with certain processes, visual cues, and motifs that come back over and over—the cycles of plants and associated creatures, leaves, certain tree species, seeds, multiples of lines and shapes."

Her experience with the work is enriched by her love of literature and a proclivity for connecting literature and poetry with some of her pieces. "I'm keenly interested in literature—particularly poetry. One of my favorite activities is to match a poem with one of my artworks. A quote or poem enlivens the experience for me and—I hope—for others."

"This suite continues my work with tree rings and their significance. Tree rings record time and events in the life of a tree by building layer upon layer of fresh cells, leaving the marks of its life forever preserved within. Similarly, we move through our lives collecting and sometimes burying our own memories. Like walking a labyrinth, these pieces describe the outward journey from the heart, the journey back inward, and the state of balance when both journeys are accomplished."

Go Outside

Leeft to right: Avian Heart #3 | Winter, wall hanging from Woven Woods | Lorraine's studio | *Gypsy Moth*, 2019, framed textile

Be inside the inside itself.

Don't hold this thought

That you are journeying toward something,

Because that itself is an admission

That you're outside somewhere.

What you are searching for is already what you are.

—Mooji

Lorraine Roy earned a bachelor of science degree in agriculture from the University of Ontario, majoring in ornamental horticulture. She has been studying developments in tree research since graduating and has been working full time with textiles for more than thirty years. The focus of her work is trees and the myriad connections they have with each other, with other organisms, and with humans. She creates wall hangings and framed textiles by using raw-edge machine-appliqué techniques and embroidery. Lorraine draws on her background in science to create images in fabric that evoke the strong connection she feels with the natural world. Most of her wall pieces are inspired by the biology, mythology, and symbolism of trees, classic emblems of the communion of earth and spirit. She is the recipient of several grants from the Canada Council and the Ontario Arts Council and has taught and lectured across Canada, and her work has been shown internationally and throughout Canada. Lorraine lives and works in Dundas, Ontario, Canada.

Lorraine's curiosity for topics outside art itself has added depth to her work. She suggests, "Choose one subject or motif that you feel passion for, something well outside the art curriculum, and study it to the greatest breadth and depth possible." This practice has served Lorraine well. Even if you are not involved in full-time art making, she suggests that you step outside today. Find something in nature, such as a leaf or plant, bring it in, and learn all you can about it. Something you learn could spark even more study or a theme that you want to explore.

If you feel disconnected from the natural environment around you, use science to close that gap and make a fundamental shift in how you live and consider your part in the larger ecosystem.

1. HJ Andrews Experimental Forest: Long-Term Ecological Research, https://andrewsforest.oregonstate.edu.

2. "Hidden Partners: Mycorrhizal Fungi and Plants," NYBG herbarium intern Matthew Pace, International Plant Science Center, C. V. Starr Virtual Herbarium, New York Botanical Garden, https://sciweb.nybg.org/science2/hcol/mycorrhizae.asp.html.

Frank Kraljic
SPACE . . . THE FINAL FRONTIER

"Witnessing the solar corona blossom around the moon's disc after completely obscuring the sun is nevertheless a soulfully moving event. One can vicariously admire and appreciate the spectacle through photography, videos, and stories of past solar eclipses, but none will replace the awe, grandeur, and inspiration of that experience for yourself . . . from the disappearance of our star, the drop in temperature, the stillness of surrounding life, and the reactions of those around you."

Frank Kraljic savors the time he spends outside his home in Arizona on a clear evening, his telescope and camera at hand.

During the day, he is engrossed in managing his media production company, which includes regularly filming in the US and in several other countries. Spending time with the night sky gives Frank a release. It offers a freedom that defies words; it's transcendent. "In those moments, I feel safe, comfortable, and even meditative. I am able to disappear in those times. I can put aside everything else that is going on in the world and in my life," he said. Frank's attraction to the night sky started many years ago, in Flagstaff, Arizona. He had snuck into his grandmother's room and, noticing the images on the television, was instantly mesmerized by the launch of the first US space shuttle.

He was only three years old at the time, but that early memory stuck with him. There were several rounds of thunderstorms moving through Arizona that day, but the sky was crystal clear at Kennedy Space Center, Cape Canaveral, Florida. "From that day on, I was captivated by the sky and wondered what was up there. I spent my childhood drawing, taking pictures, and making little movies, all about science. As unlikely as it seems, my father kept encouraging me to become an artist versus a scientist!"

Fast-forward to Frank as a teenager, when he was offered an internship with NASA related to the Galileo mission to Jupiter, connecting him, once again, to Cape Canaveral. The internship involved studying two asteroids that the Galileo spacecraft had passed on its way to Jupiter. He continued that research for a couple of years while also pursuing his interest in artwork and drawing.

Frank was a loyal Star Trek Trekkie, with a lifelong admiration for Captain Kirk. He also lionized Indiana Jones. "I take the character traits from those childhood heroes and apply them to everything in my life—being daring, being the nerd in the academic setting, but also being the real-life adventurer seeking the things that are important to me and my studies. Many friends call me Indiana Frank."

Frank's early experience worked together with his penchant for exploring the universe and imagining new worlds. He was in awe of the vastness of the universe. Looking at photos of the sky taken by others was not enough for young Frank. Seeing the sky for himself was critical. "I can look at images of a pretty beach or landscape, but that never substitutes for actually spending time in far-flung locations myself, so it follows that looking through the telescope observationally helped me witness things myself, in the moment. That is still true today." Ever since high school, wherever he has gone, Frank has taken time to photograph the night sky. "Astral photography has always been part of my life."

Frank was sixteen when the release of the movie *The Lion King* inspired him to pursue animation and film. His career path took him right into a community college film program, although planetary science continued to hold his attention, as did studying the night sky.

For the next several years, he worked as an editor while starting his own production company, Deep Sky Films, in 2001. During that time, he began directing commercials, won an Emmy Award, and built his business. He gradually moved from editing to producing and directing. His travels have taken him to many

In daytime we investigate but at night we believe.

—*Henry James Slack, "Conversation V: A Journey by Night," in* The Ministry of the Beautiful

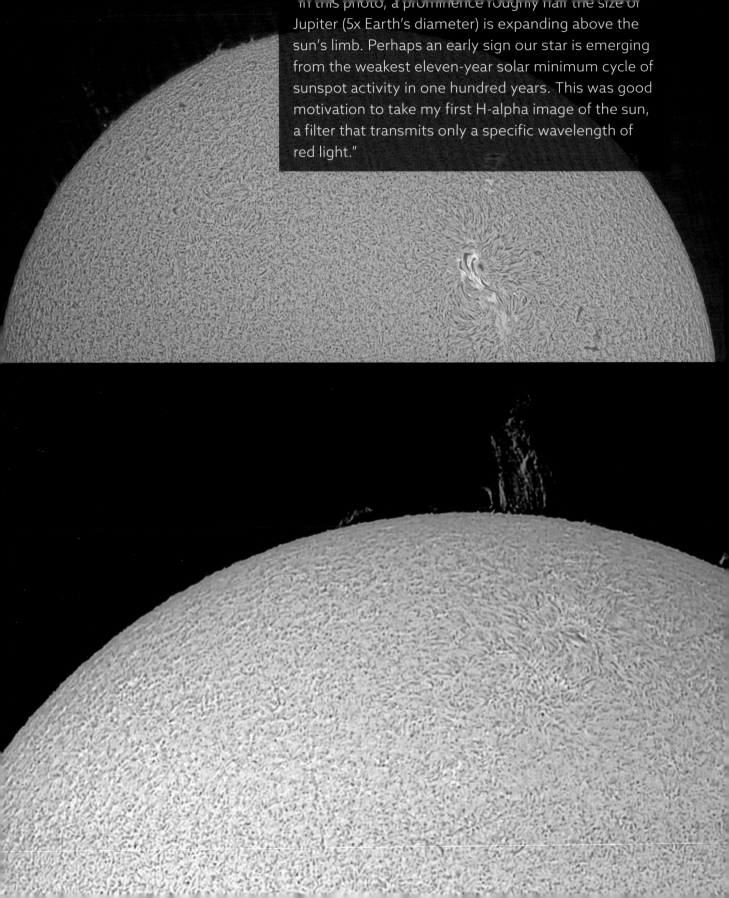

In this photo, a prominence roughly half the size of Jupiter (5x Earth's diameter) is expanding above the sun's limb. Perhaps an early sign our star is emerging from the weakest eleven-year solar minimum cycle of sunspot activity in one hundred years. This was good motivation to take my first H-alpha image of the sun, a filter that transmits only a specific wavelength of red light."

"I have chosen the path of planetary photography in addition to deep-sky photography because it goes back to my roots of exploring new worlds. There are numerous planets in our neighborhood; each one is special and different. Being able to observe and photograph them helps me explore them. For example, I can watch dust storms evolve in real time on Mars. And witness live volcanoes on the surface of the sun. It's amazing!"

places, but time spent in Africa and Afghanistan in particular helped him develop documentary and docu-style directing and cinematography skills. All along, he has been tracking and photographing the nightscape while also pursuing one of his heart projects: following virus hunters who are seeking out the origin of the Ebola virus. "I have been to thirty-five countries, including three or four war zones and into other insecure places, looking for the most dangerous virus in the world," he said.

In 2014, Frank had just returned from the front lines of the Ebola outbreak. He was recuperating from his trip by hiking in Arizona's Petrified Forest National Park, when he learned about the National Park Service (NPS) artist-in-residence program. "I had always been enamored of the Petrified Forest and its geologic history, and I was amazed by the combination of the stark landscape and the nightscape. I pitched doing nightscape photography in the Petrified Forest for my project and was accepted into the program. My work as an artist in residence was to feature the night sky along with the landscape, bringing the two together. In those images, the night sky became the background for the Petrified Forest itself."

That is when Frank pursued his mastery of nightscape photography in earnest, everything from creating the exposures to painting the landscape with light, with dramatic results. "In the early days, the compositing or processing of astronomical photography was very basic; astral photography was a new thing." Frank utilized his time at the Petrified Forest to refine his technical skills in astral photography.

Frank has built three telescopes and has had several articles published in *Astronomy* magazine. His keen observational skills and knowledge of celestial events led the way for expanding his study to planetary photography. For example, he was able to ascertain when it was the best time to photograph the Milky Way, Jupiter, or the phases of the sun. In Frank's words, "I am captivated by understanding celestial events, such as planetary conjunctions, which is when a couple of planets, although they are not next to each other in space, look like they are right next to each other to the naked eye. Also, lunar eclipses, planets, and other dramatic celestial happenings offer unlimited opportunities for discovery. I try to find stunning landscapes to photograph that complement the dramatic happenings in the night sky. For example, I photographed the solar eclipse in Chile in July 2019. I was able to travel to one of the observatories there and capture that amazing event."

Arcing beyond the upper left limb of the sun is an enormous stream of incandescent ionized gas called a prominence. The sun is the most dynamic body in our solar system. Features such as prominences noticeably change or evolve over the course of several minutes. Some solar-specific telescopes filter through only the red light emitted by hydrogen, referred to as H-alpha. Over the next few years, we can expect more activity on the sun's surface as our star approaches the peak of its eleven-year solar activity cycle, caused by the magnetic poles flipping. The next great American total solar eclipse will occur during the sun's peak activity, which will provide an incredible visual display.

Nighttime rock formation in the Petrified Forest National Park, Arizona

Nighttime rock formation in the Petrified Forest National Park, Arizona

"The night sky is like therapy; it's like home. I go out with my telescope a couple of times a month. I'm still out there to witness things for myself, but being under the night sky—there is something that fundamentally resonates with the cognitive, mental side, as well as the spiritual side of me, deep within me. I am able to disappear into the universe. I can live on the earth but explore beyond the earth. It could be analogous to people who find a mental refuge in painting or doing yoga. They find that space that separates them from the world, giving them clarity of mind and body. That is what the night sky—the universe—does for me."

Frank's early vision of heroic explorers and space travel, his worldwide travels for work and adventuring, and the deep knowledge of astronomy that he has fostered for so long work together to inform the role that astronomy and, more specifically, skyscape photography play in his life now. The technical and whimsical parts of him have become a vehicle for the spiritual aspects of Frank's life. "Every year Jupiter is high in our night sky, and every year there is something new and different. The red spot has been shrinking, storms come and go, its features are ever changing. The belts of Jupiter are changing saturation and hues. The depth of the colors changes and sometimes they disappear altogether. Saturn is the same. Sometimes storms evolve, emerge, and pop. They are transient. They appear for a week or two, then disappear. A storm can last a year or a few days. These

phenomena come and go. It is amazing to observe and photograph something that is ever changing."

Despite being involved in the film industry, Frank continues to make his home in Arizona, where they have three hundred days of sunshine a year, which equals three hundred clear nights, when he can walk out of his house and be able to look up and see stars. "That is the number one reason why I haven't moved to Hollywood or to a skiing location, when skiing is something I love. I want to always find the night sky. It gives me solace."

Until the 16th century, naked-eye comets such as the summer of 2020's comet NEOWISE were considered by many cultures as bad omens. History would later prove otherwise. Although one could argue a connection between this comet and the events of 2020, NEOWISE's presence in the sky was a highlight to a dim year. The night I took this picture, hundreds of spectators representing many demographics gathered every night off the highway ramps at Sunset Point on the I-17 north of Phoenix to observe the comet during its weeklong peak. Strangers directed newcomers where to look. Some shared binoculars or pictures from their digital camera. The people had gathered to experience something special, and for that moment we all shared something positive in common.

Note: The short streak above left of the comet shown here is a meteor, which is generally a small rock from space burning up in Earth's atmosphere about 60 miles up. NEOWISE at the time of this picture was around 60,000,000 miles away.

Go Outside

For someone who has an interest in astronomy or astral photography but has never had anyone introduce them to either one, Frank has a recommendation. He encourages finding a place free from light pollution and spend time really looking at the night sky. "Allow yourself to feel its magnificence. Just drive out of the city. I go out at night in the middle of the desert and look at the night sky. I haven't been abducted by aliens yet!"

In 1977, lightning from a severe thunderstorm struck a power plant at Indian Point, New York. The result was a sudden power failure that plunged all of New York City into darkness. It was the first time that many New Yorkers had ever really seen the night sky. For Frank, this is appalling. "I think it is important for everyone to get out of the city and see the night sky. When the brownout happened in New York City, it was the first time many New Yorkers had ever seen the Milky Way."

Frank Kraljic has pursued astral and planetary photography since childhood. His professional life as the owner of an Emmy Award–winning media production company augments his passion for astronomical explorations and photography. He also is an extreme sportsman, spending much of his time spelunking, power paragliding, and hiking, among other sports. He considers himself an avid worldwide adventurer. A graduate of Arizona State University's film program, Frank still makes his home in Arizona, where he can continue to explore the night skies.

Right: Examining the night sky with a Transformational Tools and Technologies (TTT) telescope

"Start by getting as far away from light pollution as you can. Take an hour to drive out of the city if you are in an urban setting. It takes about twenty to forty minutes for your eyes to fully adjust to the dark. Look at the sky, experience the universe that we live in. Take the next step by photographing it, or buy a telescope and give it a try. Then you can explore the other galaxies to see for yourself what is out there.

The night sky is a natural resource. We have explored almost every inch of this planet. For humanity to grow, we need to embrace that our future is out *there*. Also, fundamentally, as self-aware human beings, understanding our place in the universe is so important. I know many people who, despite being very religious, are uninformed as to where we are, the scope of the universe, and how we fit into it. It's important to understand our own planet's relationship to the Milky Way, which is home to hundreds of billions of stars and planets. That's just *our* galaxy. So, going out into the night sky is the first step. Asking yourself, 'I wonder what is out there?' is the first step to opening this door and pursuing an understanding of the universe we live in. That in itself is a spiritual experience."

Carrie Anne K'iinuwaas Vanderhoop
LIVING YOUR LEGACY

Creating weavings is personally and culturally significant because it contributes to the cultural revitalization and decolonization of the Haida. My weavings serve as an unbroken link to my ancestors. The regalia that I create is worn by performers who dance, sing, and drum at Potlatches and other Indigenous celebrations.

—Tiffany S'idluujaa Vanderhoop

Naaxiin dance cape
Materials: merino wool, yellow cedar, sea otter fur
Back design: Ghost Face
Earrings: gold eagles by Aay Aay Hans
Woven in 2014
Photo: Danielle Louise

Most people have some push and pull in their lives. They are stretching in one direction at the expense of another, or they have inner conflicts that seem to be the same this year as they were last year or the year before.

Carrie Anne is one of the few people I have ever met who has brought together every aspect of her life to honor and be in alignment with her core beliefs and culture. When asked about any aspect of her life, Carrie Anne's replies lead—either directly or indirectly—back to her connection to community, to the land, and to her ancestry.

As the daughter of an Aquinnah Wampanoag father from Noepe (Martha's Vineyard), Massachusetts, and Haida mother from Haida Gwaii, British Columbia, Carrie Anne is the beneficiary of a rich Native history. She lives out the legacy of her forebears even as she fosters the independent direction of her own life. The Haida are matrilineal, part of the Masset Inlet Eagle clan. The traditional Haida Gwaii territory encompasses parts of southern Alaska, the archipelago of Haida Gwaii, and its surrounding waters. Their precontact population was in the tens of thousands in several dozen towns dispersed throughout the islands. During the time of contact, the population fell to about six hundred due to introduced diseases including measles, typhoid, and smallpox. Today, Haida people make up half of the 5,000 people living on the islands.[1]

Carrie Anne spent much of her childhood in Aquinnah. "Aquinnah does not have many people. Growing up I could walk from one side to the other and any house I passed was the home of friends or family. It's a quiet community with beautiful beaches." Many places on Martha's Vineyard have been renamed, embracing hackneyed tropes such as ghost stories, tales of haunted swamps, and buried treasure. "I want people to know

these places and how special they are, not the renaming and demonizing of them. These places and their stories tell us how to care for our land. When I am in Aquinnah, every place I go, there are stories I have heard from my childhood that connect me to those places. Those stories of the land make me feel like I am home when I am there. I am not just there, I am a *part* of that place, just like the grass, the berries, and the deer," she said.

Carrie Anne ultimately settled on the land of her mother's tribe, Haida Gwaii, a series of islands, coastal bays, and inlets off the coast of British Columbia. Carrie Anne is a member of a weaving family. Traditionally, Haida women made a range of baskets, from large coarsely woven ones that would allow clams to drain, to drinking cups so tightly woven they would hold water.[2] In Carrie Anne's case, she concentrates her weaving on Raven's Tail and naaxiin textiles. Naaxiin (naheen) is the word used by the Haida and Tlingit for the form-line-designed chief's robe now commonly referred to as chilkat. Raven's Tail, the predecessor to the chilkat weaving tradition, was named for the resemblance it bore to the tail feathers of a raven. Unlike an actual raven's tail, it is more minimalistic, with black-and-white geometric designs. In contrast, chilkat robes combine imagery from nature with "form line" motifs common throughout Northwest Coast traditional art.[3] Carrie Anne's weavings are unadulterated by current themes

1. Council of the Haida Nation, haidanation.ca.

2. Canadian Museum of History, historymuseum.ca.

3. Native Arts & Cultures Foundation, nativeartsandcultures.org.

The most important
education I have
received is from
community, family,
and the land.
—Carrie Anne
K'iinuwaas
Vanderhoop

and changes. Her vision is carried out through the sophisticated, geometric designs and motifs passed down to her from her ancestors.

She also weaves items from cedar bark and gathers and prepares spruce tree roots that grow along the sandy beaches of Haida Gwaii. For generations, the women in her family have been weavers, and now Carrie Anne is teaching her daughter. "I remember watching my great-grandmother weave and being taught how to gather the materials from the forest. When I was a child, and even today, we practice mindfulness in the woods, allowing no negative thoughts or feelings, keeping our senses open. We also embrace natural forest management. For example, we were taught not to go to the same part of the forest twice. It's important to follow these practices because of the relationship we have with the forest; everything is interconnected."

Carrie Anne laments the decline of yellow cedar trees along the Northwest Coast as a result of climate change. "What happens when we don't have those resources anymore? It is critical that we pay attention to the signs and tell stories to young people that will help us move into the future, not just our own old stories, but stories of what is happening to the yellow cedar today and other threats to our waters, traditional foods, and medicines.

"We have an ongoing relationship with the neighboring tribes and nations along the coast. We were dependent on our neighbors for sharing resources. For example, mountain goat fur was considered a big trade item, almost like a currency. There were no mountain goats on Haida Gwaii, so we traded for that resource. People regularly traveled along the coast by canoe. There were even some central places along the coast between the villages where people would gather. Spruce root was another big trade item. On Haida Gwaii there are long stretches of sandy beaches where spruce roots extend in straight lengths. In most other places along the coast, the spruce trees grow around craggy shorelines around rocks and cliffs, making the roots not ideal to weave with." Carrie Anne conveys how those kinds of extended relationships have always run through the lives of the Haida, enriching their deep respect for life's interconnectedness.

As Carrie Anne grew up, she became aware that the adults in her life outside her community had low expectations when it came to education. She refused to be minimized and treated as just another statistic or a stereotype. Instead, she used those feelings to her advantage when applying to the University of Massachusetts. "The summer before I graduated from high school, I was completely focused. I worked hard all summer long, so I could earn some money, and was preparing myself to attend university and be successful. I got through the first year, and it went so smoothly. I thought it would be really hard and I wasn't going to be smart enough, but I ended up enjoying it so much more than high school!"

Despite being pleased with her transition to college, Carrie Anne encountered racism toward Indigenous people. She consistently treated those times as an opportunity to speak. Gaining a voice became an integral part of her education. She was struck by the lack of content around Indigenous peoples' history and culture and that they were not represented in any of the literature courses she was taking. "There wasn't one course in my program of study that I could take that focused on any Indigenous life or introduced those themes in the assigned literature. Also, in my experience in education in general, I understood that I was never the audience that this experience was intended for. I thought about the way that I learn, what is important to me, and my values. That's when I started to take education classes, because I wanted to be part of a change and wanted to imagine and work toward a curriculum that could be inclusive of different perspectives and worldviews."

Carrie Anne has a complex relationship with her experience in academia. She sees her accomplishments themselves as a kind of resistance against the ideas that were fed to her in her childhood about dropout rates in aboriginal communities. That is, during her academic career, she wondered why the curriculum was not more inclusive of a wider audience, including more expansive content, such as incorporating literature from Indigenous people. "I didn't understand why it felt like education largely reflected only a Western worldview," she said. Ultimately, she was able to proactively build her master's degree plan to at least partially mitigate the narrow content and focus that had been presented to her.

Carrie Anne's life path informs her ability to live authentically in several settings and observe how each culture relates to others and its surroundings. Unlike her academic experience, both of her family's Native cultures are imbued with relationships to the land and to each other.

After Carrie Anne graduated from Harvard, she took the position of education director at the Wampanoag Tribe of Gay Head Aquinnah. "I wanted to give back and support the young people in my community on their educational journeys." Her message is very clear: she wants her community members to know that they can experience what is perceived as success in the mainstream academic world while they honor their heritage and build a life in their home community.

During her time at the University of Massachusetts, she wrote a play titled *Raven Prince*. It was a theatrical production that included dance, poetry, and music. She wrote, directed, and sewed costumes together with members of the local Indigenous community. It highlighted the diversity of different peoples from the Eastern Woodlands, the Northwest Coast, and other Indigenous groups. I was a Fancy Shawl and an Eastern Traditional dancer. A group of us students at UMass used to visit local schools to give performances and talk about who we are as Indigenous people."

Between her two degrees, Carrie Anne was an apprentice weaver with her mother in Washington State

Naaxiin headdress in progress, 2021

Design: Spirit Face

Materials: merino wool, yellow cedar bark

Photo: Danielle Louise

Raven's Tail robe

Woven by master weaver Evelyn Vanderhoop, Carrie Anne Vanderhoop, and Tiffany Vanderhoop.

This robe is a special four-generation robe. Carrie Anne's sister Tiffany was pregnant with her third child while they were weaving, and the older children, who were barely two years old, were always nearby watching and playing and sometimes pulling on the warp and weft. Naanii Delores came to visit Old Massett from Ketchikan, Alaska, and spent time weaving with them as well.

Commissioned by the Canadian Museum of History, 2011

Central designs: All My Ancestors, Tides, Lattice, Diamonds

Side design: Tree Shadows

Material: merino wool

on the Olympic Peninsula, traveling with her to the different villages along the Northwest Coast as a teaching assistant, and she also had the opportunity to study with her mother in museums throughout the US and Canada, and even the British Museum in London. Carrie Anne knew how important weaving was to her identity and her family's legacy, and since spending a summer on Haida Gwaii to join her mother and Naanii (grandmother) in weaving the first Raven's Tail robe that had been woven there in more than two hundred years, she knew she wanted to weave the Northwest Coast wool textile regalia.

During her apprenticeship, she was given a weaving commission to weave a traditional Raven's Tail chief's robe. That weaving continued throughout her time at Harvard University and was a way to keep her connected to her heritage while she lived in Cambridge, Massachusetts, and earned her second degree. "When I was accepted to Harvard, I had to pack up my things and go. I took the commission with me to Cambridge and continued weaving it while I was going to school. It helped ground me [and] remind me of who I was, why I was there, what I was doing, and to stay focused. Especially in such an intense program in that prestigious school, it helped me stay grounded. The loom took up so much space, but it was worth it. I pushed hard to finish it so I could wear it to the graduation ceremony. My family friend, who commissioned the robe, was happy and proud that it would be worn for that ceremony."

Carrie Anne is quick to remark that weaving the Raven's Tail robe provided an education that was equally or more valuable to her than her degrees. "I wore it to my Harvard University graduation ceremony. The traditional knowledge passed along through the weaving is from my ancestors. It represents another master's degree to me."

Most of her weaving concentrates on Native regalia, woven with wool. "I also occasionally work in cedar bark and prepare spruce root material for weaving, but I mainly weave textile garments." She is currently finishing a headdress, and her mom is currently weaving her fourth naaxiin robe. Throughout Carrie Anne's life, she has worked together with her mother on almost every large-scale project that her mother has taken on. It has been a lifetime of education and learning that continues today. Now Carrie Anne is turning her own skills around and teaching her daughter and nieces, which she finds enormously gratifying. The technical skills, creativity, and ritualized designs all come together, along with an intentional mindset while weaving. "It's important to use this time to recall our stories and celebrate our culture."

Carrie Anne continues to integrate those priorities into her professional life. She has been doing curriculum design work for several years now. She has taught at all levels, from primary to secondary and postsecondary. Her current focus is on building programs and curriculum that are antiracist, highlight Indigenous cultural safety and social justice issues, are inclusive, and also recognize hidden curricula and how to change it. "For example, my own experience had to do with what was *not* being taught. There was an erasure of so much rich, important knowledge that should be taught," she said. The Haida Gwaii Institute courses and programming include land and resource management, as well as programming in marine and terrestrial sciences. "We blend Indigenous knowledge systems and work with traditional ecological wisdom also, while making sure the programming is benefiting the community."

She also recently authored the children's book titled *Seeqan, Neepun, Keepun, Pap8n, Aquinnah Seasons* (Tradewind Books), which is written from a Wampanoag perspective. With this project and in all things, Carrie Anne is true to her core identity and life's path. "I highlighted our connection with nature, family, community, food, wildlife, and sea life that I see and that our people have had a relationship with, since time immemorial." Carrie Anne's life is a conduit for the ancient wisdom and teachings of her ancestors, which she passes along in the way she inhabits the world.

Carrie Anne's most profound vehicle for sharing the legacy of her heritage and its interrelationship with the land, the people, and her ancestors is through weaving. She said, "I am a weaver. Everything I do comes from that core of me, and everything I do is in relation to the land and carrying that knowledge forward."

Go Outside

Carrie Anne approaches everyday life with a sense of wonder. "As for getting outside and connecting to nature to nurture creativity, be curious, live in awe like a child, watch all the tiny things. Close your eyes and listen, make friends with plants and resident birds or other wildlife, be an observer, imagine the history of the place and the Indigenous peoples whose territory you are on. Consider the future of the place and how we might be impacting that future. Think about what the natural world around us provides, how it sustains us, and then think about how we can have a reciprocal relationship with the environment.

"Find a favorite spot and become part of it. As a Haida weaver, how I was taught and what I saw with my Naanii [grandmother] and aunties when entering the forest to gather weaving materials or food or medicine is that it is so important to clear your mind and be present. Use all your senses to listen, see, and feel the forest and environment around you. It can be dangerous,

Carrie Anne K'iinuwaas Vanderkoop's father is Aquinnah Wampanoag, from Noepe (Martha's Vineyard), Massachusetts, and her mother is Haida from Old Masset, Haida Gwaii. She belongs to the Gawa Git'ans, Masset Inlet Eagle clan. Coming from a family with a strong weaving legacy, she is a weaver of cedar bark and is also a Raven's Tail and naaxiin (chilkat) textile weaver. Naaxiin is the word used by the Haida and Tlingit for the form-line-designed chief's robe now commonly referred to as chilkat. Carrie Anne studied comparative literature and sociology at the University of Massachusetts Amherst, where she earned her BA. She went on to earn a master's degree from Harvard University's Graduate School of Education, where she focused her studies on multicultural education and the sociology of schools. She also works as the academic lead for the Haida Gwaii Higher Education Society. In her spare time, Carrie Anne enjoys adventures with her daughter in the great outdoors.

so be mindful of the potential to be harmed or cause harm. You have to have respect for everything and an understanding that everything is interconnected. When we gather cedar bark or roots for weaving, we think about what we intend to use the material for. There is expressed intent. We ask the tree, we thank the tree, and we leave the place as much as we found it as possible, leaving the outer cedar bark that is removed from the tree face up on the ground so that the new, lighter, exposed side doesn't stand out. We replace the moss and grass that gets disturbed when we gather roots to hide the root paths that get uncovered. We only take what is needed and use it with gratitude."

Left to right: Weaving with mother, Evelyn Vanderhoop, on current naaxiin chief's robe project, 2021 | Naanii Delores Churchill 2006 National Endowment for the Arts Award recipient, portrait with granddaughters. *From left to right:* Tiffany Vanderhoop, Paula Varnell, Carrie Anne Vanderhoop, Delores Churchill, Teresa May Varnell, Gloria Burns. | Headdress woven by Carrie Anne, Shawl woven by Evelyn Vanderhoop

Kari Lønning
DELIGHTING IN NATURE'S RHYTHMS

I am a maker of objects. What I do comes from a passion born out of curiosity, problem-solving, and a love of color and architecture. My hands bring to life what I see around me and things from my imagination.

—*Kari Lønning*

Center detail of *Rain Music*, a hairy basket for the wall

For Kari Lønning, basketry was a natural combination of two passions: ceramics and weaving.

The sculptural forms of ceramics and the textures of weaving came together in her basketmaking practice, also satisfying her yearning to work in three dimensions.

Kari has made her living from her art for more than forty years, an admirable and rare accomplishment. According to Kari, "When I first started, I never thought I'd be able to make a living making and selling baskets. I used to make wooden puzzles, then quilts. But baskets just hit all the right points for me—the color, form, texture, volume . . . I don't separate work from play, which gives me an advantage over a lot of people. I don't necessarily need vacations. I love what I do."

I have admired Kari's work for years at museums and at the semiannual Craft Boston event sponsored by the Society of Arts + Crafts, but when I first caught a glimpse of her pieces next to the environments that they are based on, I instantly gained a greater understanding of how she experiences the world around her. However, rather than beginning with a particular scene in mind, Kari's inspirations simmer in her subconscious. When asked about her pairings of landscapes to baskets, she says, "I actually work kind of backward. I'm very aware of the colors around me and in the places I visit. I'm sensitive to the colors at different times of the year. Rather than doing an entire color scheme to go with the garden, I just start dyeing the colors. In time, I can see that the colors were the inspiration, but I don't know that until I'm finished.

"I enjoy working with my hands, interacting with the materials. I handle, gather, dye, and weave the material. I work free-form with just simple tools, such as an awl,

scissors, pliers, and a knife. I love seeing a basket develop from nothing into a form with color and movement."

Kari spent many of her childhood summers on Hesnesøya, a small island on the southeastern coast of Norway. Many years ago, it was a convenient stopping place for sailors traveling the coast of Norway. Her grandparents bought what used to be the tavern. They had a cluster of houses there, and she spent her time walking on the rocky perimeter, fishing with the family, and gathering treasures from nature. It's now a favorite vacation mooring and hiking spot for vacationers traveling the coastline. She and her sister still own a house on the island and spend time there during the summer.

As a result of her childhood experiences, Kari enjoys living inside and outside. A passion for nature cuts to the heart of what Scandinavians call *friluftsliv*, and Kari certainly embraces friluftsliv in her own life on her one-third acre in southeastern Connecticut. She has utilized every bit of it to create garden rooms, replete with wandering pathways, connecting one area to another. Most of its paths meander through perennials, bushes, and trees. The recent addition of a greenhouse has given her even more potential for growing and tending to the nature that surrounds her home. Kari moved into the house in 1979 and started planting small areas on the lot right away. "I built up each area. Now I can barely plant a bulb without hitting another plant!"

Kari is best known for her hand-dyed "hairy" rattan baskets, where she inserts hundreds of short pieces of reed while she weaves up the sides of her baskets. Even after several years of reading and writing about basketry, I have

Nature does not hurry,
yet everything is
accomplished.

—Lao-Tzu

Left: Sea and Beaches, dyed rattan reed

Right: Inspiration from the plants at the Chicago Botanic Garden

never seen her technique used by other artists. Kari uses a multi-element twining technique to achieve her complex spiral and vertical patterns, which creates depth and movement. To achieve patches of contrasting color, she uses a form of tapestry weaving. If you have ever attempted to make a basket—or watched anyone else work a basket from that first circle in the base, weaving around and around building up the base, then gradually weaving up the sides, you'll have an under-standing of what an admirable feat of dexterity it is. Kari increases this inherent complexity by adding her "hairy" pieces for texture, as she weaves up the sides of each basket.

Due to her years of basketmaking experience, she understands the math needed to achieve patterns that suggest waves or clouds. From a technical standpoint, she accomplishes these effects by changing the number of weavers or spokes. Weaving with multiple weavers at the same time gives her the ability to change out different colors, creating the subtle gradations found in sunsets and shadows. She uses her training in textiles to dye her own reed. Being able to dye infinite shades of color gives her the ability to respond to the colors around her as nature and the seasons change.

Kari's daily routine includes time spent in the garden and at least two hikes. On one of those hikes, she tripped over a vine along the ground. It did not break, so she investigated it and found that it was akebia, a vine that is invasive in the Northeast. That hike was the beginning of a new direction in her work, as it revealed what, for Kari, turned out to be the riches of akebia. "I'm a park ranger for this area. The local Open Space and Watershed Land Acquisition Department officials have tried to get rid of akebia by burning it, covering it, and smothering it, but they couldn't get rid of it. They think it's very funny that I'm making artwork out of it."

Kari enjoys how strong, thin, and flexible akebia is. "I can do all the complex patterns I usually do, and it can be dyed should I want more color. However, akebia offers various colors, including different shades of brown, green, and the white from stripping the bark from the vine." Many of the colors are related to the age of the vine and the time of year when she picks it. Using the stripped akebia ensures that the color contrast will stay, even as the piece ages. "On my walks, I tend to spend an extra forty-five minutes pulling vines. It's like collecting shells on a beach. Some vines are up to 15 feet long. Some of it goes into the trees, but in my area it's mostly a ground cover."

Kari learned how to make two-ply cord using natural materials in Denmark where she was teaching at the

> **Friluftsliv**
> (pronounced free-loofts-leev)
>
> *A term used to broadly describe Norwegians' passion for nature. It was first coined by Norwegian poet Henrik Ibsen and literally translates as "free air's life."*

Left: Half Akebia Melon. Akebia vine melon basket woven using tapestry techniques.

Below: Color inspiration from the Norwegian landscape

Above: Bouquets of Norwegian wildflowers are often inspiration for baskets and serve as an emotional connection with nature.

Right: Hairy vessel form made from artist-dyed rattan reed

Exposed Spoke Series #2. Akebia vines, dyed rattan, and encaustic medium.

Color inspiration discovered in a Norwegian farm market

Color inspiration discovered in a Norwegian farm market

Danish Association of Willow Basketmakers Conference in 2017, learning how to make grasses and vines into rope. Upon returning to the US, she and Willy, her 104-pound Old English sheepdog, resumed their forays into the woods. It was on one of these outings that she tripped over an akebia vine. "It didn't break!" Unlike Virginia creeper, wisteria, honeysuckle, ivy, or other vines often used in basketmaking, akebia had really strong tensile strength and wonderful flexibility. Clearly, the confluence of her new skills along with literally stumbling upon the akebia sparked a new creative direction.

Akebia quinata was brought to the United States from Asia in the late 1800s as a decorative plant. Unfortunately, it acclimated so well that its aggressive growth habit smothered our native plants. In most areas it is classified as an invasive species. "Because conservationists consider it a thug, I am free to collect as much as I want or need."

Kari always knew that she wanted to make things. She began her career as a potter, where she was drawn to the physicality of creating vessel forms in clay, but her Virgo nature was drawn to the technical processes and the immediate use of color available in weaving. Basketry was the solution, a union of her two passions. "Being mostly self-taught in basketry, I've been able to experiment with techniques until I find my own design solutions. I made my first double-wall construction as a way to make the walls of a basket appear extra thick. My hairy technique was a way to make a better bird's nest for my cousin's aviary."

Kari is still gathering treasures and making containers to hold them. The windowsills and shelves of her cozy Connecticut home are replete with carefully collected and placed natural items, since she continues to be inspired by the friluftsliv of her youth.

Dyed rattan reed with Emma, Kari's Old English sheepdog

Go Outside

Kari Lønning's daily life is an ongoing conversation with the outdoors. She encourages taking the time and energy to authentically engage with your surroundings by observing changes from day to day and in different environments, and at various times within the same day. She embraces the nature of friluftsliv, to regularly experience slow, flow, and peak experiences in nature.

"There is a lot of interaction with what I see and hear as I walk. I wait and watch for different plants, which bloom in different seasons or on other trails. Right now, I'm looking forward to seeing the sweet, blue-purple flowers of wild hepatica. I found two plants growing a few years ago, so this year I built three-pointed, stick tepees over them, so they don't get accidentally crushed by passersby." Kari hikes at different times of the day and in different directions on the same trail. She notices how shadows alter what she sees and how other small changes seem to appear.

Kari Lønning attended the University of Norway–Oslo, where she studied Norwegian crafts. She then studied textiles and ceramics at Syracuse University in New York, where she developed an interest in patterns and complex weaving techniques. Though many of her vessel forms still reflect her continued love of ceramics, basketry became the natural union of these two passions. She makes one-of-a-kind art baskets using artist-dyed rattan reed, as well as locally collected, invasive *a*kebia vines. Her baskets are in galleries and museum collections, including the Smithsonian in Washington, DC, and the US embassy in Bangkok, Thailand.

Left to right: Akebia vines grow so aggressively that they smother native plant life. | Akebia vines after the leaves have been removed and before they are hung up to dry. | 5-to-25-foot Akebia vines, with Willy for scale

Barbara Schneider
CELEBRATING NATURE'S IMPERFECTIONS

I relish the back and forth that I
am making something from
nature that can also be
interpreted as abstract. I find
beauty in unexpected places.

—*Barbara Schneider*

Line Dance, Tree Ring Patterns, var. 13. *My Corner of the World,* SAQA Midwest Views 2021

Barbara's life's work is built on a foundation of contrasting forces: celebrating the temporary and fostering a powerful legacy. Both of these things are integral to her love of nature. Her artwork is based on honoring the temporary and imperfect in nature.

In contrast to celebrating the ephemeral, the legacy that Barbara is building works in tandem with her art, as she contributes to the reforestation of conservation areas in McHenry County, Illinois.

Barbara's artwork draws attention to the inherent beauty that is often overlooked by us all as we absent-mindedly traipse through crumbling, wet leaves; walk past trees in seasonal transition; or step over a decaying, hollow log covered in an array of mosses. These subtle yet powerful changes are always at work around us. To Barbara, they typify a lifetime of exploring the Japanese concept of *wabi-sabi*, a sensibility and worldview centered on the acceptance of transience and imperfection. Barbara's mission is to capture these moments of perfect imperfection, freezing them in a particular time and place. Her artwork intensifies the small natural elements by blowing them up in scale, allowing us to recognize the essence of the subject in a new way.

Her love of wabi-sabi plays out in many ways, from the boro fabrics of Japan to the forest floors in her own community and around the world. Over the years, she has hiked coast to coast in England, across the grand traverse of the Alps, and through the Routeburn Track in Fiordland National Park in New Zealand and has traversed other areas of New Zealand as well as several places in Italy. She also regularly hikes at home and at several national and state parklands around the US.

Sometimes she delights in finding a perfect stem or flower. To Barbara, the perfect flower in a field of possibilities is the one with the most character. In her words, "I am focused on the temporary state of nature as it breaks down and transitions to another state. That ephemeral moment, such as reflections on water, are really about paying attention to a single moment. Things are constantly changing." Barbara's work plucks those exquisite moments out of thin air for us and highlights them in her work, inviting us to take notice and relish them in the same way that she does.

Barbara has created several thoughtful series through the years; all of them sit at the crossroads between her dedication to nature and the wabi-sabi aesthetic. Viewers' interpretations of her work range from abstract to realistic. At times they may start with the former in mind and, after taking a step back, realize that they are witnessing the latter. In a moment, a piece transforms from abstract painting to realistic leaf pile, and they are seeing the work again, as if for the first time. "I relish the back and forth that I am making something from nature that also can be interpreted as abstract. I find beauty in unexpected places."

While working on her ongoing series, *Reflections*: Water, she experienced an epiphany of the temporary and has been celebrating those moments ever since. "That idea of the ephemeral moment really launched my work. That has continued to play out in all my series. What the camera sees, what I see, what the viewers see, and all the connections based on something that wasn't even really there or was there for only a moment . . . I love that you're seeing and creating something that is real and at the same time never actually existed."

For Barbara's series *Leaves and Forest Floor*, which she has continued to develop over time, she explores and interprets natural images by enlarging and reshaping

I like to capture the essence of images made of light and movement, images that are infinitely variable.

—*Barbara Schneider*

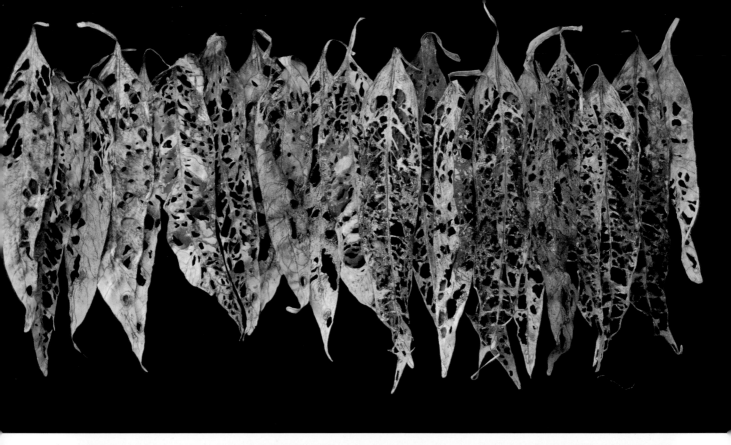

Top: Leaf Fall, var. 3 fragments. Ink jet–printed, stitched, dyed, painted, fused, shaped, cut. Assorted exhibits.

Bottom: Reflections, Venice, Fondamenta Venier, var. 21. Hand-dyed fabrics, fused, machine-stitched, based on photos from Venice. SAQA H2O.

Wabi-sabi: "Wabi" connotes rustic simplicity, freshness, or quietness and can be applied to both natural and human-made objects as an expression of understated elegance. It can also be used to refer to the quirks and anomalies that arise from the process of making things that are seen to add uniqueness and elegance to the finished object. "Sabi" refers to the beauty or serenity that comes with age, when the life of the object and its impermanence are evidenced in its patina and wear, or in any visible repairs.

them. "I collect leaves, pods, flowers, grasses, bark, branches, and anything else of interest and closely examine their structure and shape. In particular, I like to collect these natural objects at the end of summer, when they have begun to wither and fragment. Looking at them closely and enlarging them enables me to see them as sculptural objects. Shaping the pieces introduces a new element—light and shadow interacting with the folding surfaces. This dimensional work expands my view in many different directions.

Barbara's work starts with one of her regular hikes through one of twenty-seven sites in the McHenry County Conservation District, an organization that owns or manages more than 25,000 acres of open space, providing wildlife habitat preservation, educational opportunities, and recreational amenities. Its mission is to preserve, restore, and manage natural areas and open spaces for their intrinsic value and for the benefits to present and future generations.[1]

Once she identifies and photographs her subject, Barbara returns to her studio to begin the process of identifying the most powerful images and expanding their size. She then reinterprets the images for us, enlisting a variety of materials and techniques to achieve the desired results. Barbara embraces her artistic roots in surface design and combines those with her painterly approach.

Still Lifes in Indigo: Exploring the Wabi-Sabi Spirit is a series that allowed Barbara to engage with her boro fabrics in new ways. In short, boro are Japanese textiles that have been mended, patched, or stitched together. They often serve as shorthand for representing the wabi-sabi sensibility. The term is derived from the Japanese term *boroboro*, meaning something tattered or repaired. Collecting boro was instinctual to Barbara, as part of exploring wabi-sabi more deeply.

"*Still Lifes in Indigo* circles back to using some of my old Japanese boro fabrics as backgrounds to create settings for objects that contain a wabi-sabi spirit. They are explorations of texture, color, and form." When she saw them fold and unfurl in wonderful patterns and textures, she was compelled to do something, so she started making photographic setups.

"The boro would ripple down, flowing as part of the background." Barbara has a collection of objects in her home that she brought from Japan. She gathered them all up, took them with her to the studio, and set up a photo shoot to explore all of the frayed, patched textures. "I took many images over several days, then had them printed on fabric. Although the final pieces are still rather large, the *Still Lifes in Indigo* series started as a valiant attempt to work smaller!" Once the photos were printed on fabric, she heavily thread-painted the objects and added free-motion and hand stitching to the boro backgrounds. She also needle-felted some parts to basically break down the fabric in some of the areas, softening the edges and re-creating the look of old boro. That series includes forty pieces.

She started with a goal to create twenty pieces but found that she couldn't stop at that point. "It was like being a kid again, coloring and blending the colors. There is one piece that features ginkgo leaves on a (seemingly) white plate. There are probably twenty colors to create the white,

1. *McHenry County Conservation District, www.mccdistrict.org.*

Bottom: Still Life: Bound Book, var. 1. Digitally printed from artist photo, thread painted, framed, 2018.

A Walk at Nippersink Canoe Basin

Heavily wooded site

Stands of hickory all around

Young hickories

Small grass path

Brak fragments underfoot

Old hickory nuts underfoot

Small shade wildflowers peeking
out of leaf litter

Rose canes grabbing my pants legs

Feathers on the ground

A few more steps and more
feathers on ground

Cross small stream ons tones

Huge broken tree stump lying along path

Bright-green patch of skunk cabbage

White oak tree buds starting to
open far above

More stands of young hickory

Dandelion

Path circles back

Follow road down to stream

Curving stream going off northwest
and southeast

Sunshine sparkling on water

Birds overhead in trees

Back to trail start

but not one of them is actually white thread. It is the looking again, seeing the actual tone of each section, and using that observation to augment the photo." Barbara started that series about five years ago and worked on it for three years. She still adds to this series—and all her series—when she is in between projects.

Observations: Walking in Wonder is a departure from her previous work. She limited the color palette and created a series of twenty-seven hand-stitched textiles, each one an interpretation of a particular hike in the McHenry County Conservation District. They are not literal maps. Rather, they are interpretations of the spaces, taken from sketches and notes of the observations she made while spending time hiking and exploring each area. Barbara considers the labels that accompany each piece as an integral part of the series. They capture what she saw, heard, and experienced on each hike. "The labels matter as much as the art itself. They include notes that mention memorable moments, such as butterflies sitting on the top of a plant and hovering over the water, seeing the

tadpoles, three frogs jumping off a rock, or the sound of the wind in the trees."

Although Barbara is captivated by the temporal beauty of nature, at the same time she is building a legacy that will last well beyond all our lifetimes. That project began several years ago, when she started to learn about prairie restoration. She initially did some coursework and then started seed collecting for the conservation district. A decade of working with the McHenry Conservation District served as the foundation for Barbara's commitment to planting a thousand trees within five years. She is already well on her way, having planted more than five hundred trees with the help of family and friends. As they grow, she is tagging, taking measurements, gathering data, and GPS-marking the trees for the district. "The area was once covered in oak trees, and now it is down to only 5 percent. The district is trying to reconnect the areas again, from site to site. That's my place to be, out in the woods or in the prairie, doing long-distance hiking, walking, working, and observing."

Right: Line Dance, Tree Line Patterns, St. Marys, Glacier Park, MT, var. 5. Digitally printed, free-motion machine-stitched, fused, backed, two panels. Art Cloth Network, Anything Goes.

View of Barbara's studio space

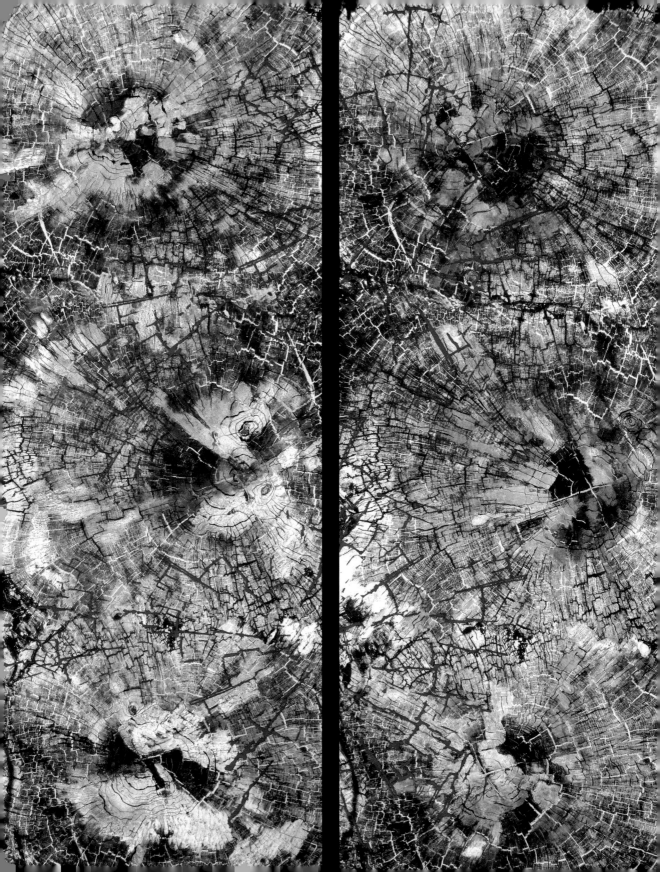

Go Outside

Barbara spends as much time as possible outside. For her *Observations: Walking in Wonder* series, she walked and rewalked the same areas and took notes about her experiences. Not only did this enrich these experiences, it meant that she built a set of memories that can be much more easily recalled because of her notes.

The next time you go outside, consider rewalking an area that you have walked before. Not every experience needs to be on a fresh hiking trail. When you visit that familiar walk, take notes as you go, and over time you can build up a notebook to remind you of the sights, sounds, and activities happening all around you, as you hike and rehike those familiar places in nature.

Barbara Schneider is an artist who uses nature as the starting point for creating sophisticated interpretations in mixed media. Her work is meant to make you view nature with new eyes. Barbara began quilting in 1996 and discovered the pleasure of working with cloth, paint, dye, and thread. Her interest in the Japanese concept of **wabi-sabi** strongly influences her work. She has an extensive background in surface design and teaches as well as exhibits nationally and internationally. Her artwork can be found both in private and public collections.

Left to right: View of Barbara's studio space | *Nippersink Canoe Basin* | *Still Life: Gingko Bowl and Boro*, var. 1. Digitally printed from artist's photo, thread painted, framed, 2016. | *Line Dance, Tree Ring Patterns*, var. 27

ACKNOWLEDGMENTS

I owe a debt of gratitude to all the artists who shared their lives with me and showed me how to live more openly, with nature as my daily guide and creative compass. As I delved deeper into the project, I found myself integrating more time in nature into my everyday life, fueled by their examples.

This project got rolling at a time when, unknowingly, I was headed for several personal challenges. Barbara Delaney and Leanne Jewett continued to review my drafts, lending their critical editorial eye and unfailing content reviews, even as I sent them in fits and starts and at all hours. The Schiffer Publishing team took over for Barbara and Leanne, consistently (and patiently) offering their insights and wisdom as they shepherded this book through the publishing process.

While I was firmly entrenched in writing about nature and creativity, Lori Butanis, Jen Moniz, Cate Prato, Beth Smith, Cami Smith, and the rest of the team at the Fiber Art Network kept plowing forward with magazine production, grants programs, calls for entry, social media and marketing development, design and layout, administrative tasks, and all the other components that have built a thriving arts organization like ours. You all have turned what was once an idea into a creative force that has become a worldwide source of inspiration and connection.

Not many authors can count on their family for professional support. Abby, you lent your unique organizational expertise as well as your insights. Nick, you resolved technical challenges and logged hours of discussion time about how nature affects the brain and increases our well-being. Mike, you are my true companion, collaborator, and partner in crime. I learn more from all my adventures when my family members are part of them, including my extended, stepped, in-lawed, and nuclear.

"The root of joy is gratefulness…
It is not joy that makes us grateful;
it is gratitude that makes us joyful."

— *Brother David Steindl-Rast*

RESOURCES

Artists

Maleah Bretz
etsy.com/shop/wovenbyleah
@wovenbyleah

James Brunt
etsy.com/uk/shop/jamesbruntartist
@jamesbruntartist
Facebook: jamebruntartist

Bethan Burton
journalingwithnature.com, naturejournalingweek.com
@journalingwithnature
Facebook: journalingwithnature
Podcast: *Journaling with Nature*

Judith Content
judithcontent.com
@Judith_Content
Other: www.craftinamerica.org

Nicole Dextras
nicoledextras.com
@ndextras

Alice Fox
alicefox.co.uk
@alicefoxartist
Facebook: alicefoxartist
Twitter: alicefoxartist

Jan Hopkins
janhopkinsart.blogspot.com
@janhopkinsart

Munir Jones
expressionsbymunir.etsy.com
@expressionsbymunir

Frank Kraljic
@fjkraljic

Kari Lonning
karibaskets.com
@karibaskets

Nick Neddo
nickneddo.com
@nick.neddo.eartharts

Lorraine Roy
lroyart.com
@lroy.art

Barbara Schneider
barbaraschneider-artist.com, barbaraschneider-artist.
blogspot.com, artclothnetwork.com, saqa.com
Facebook: CreatingWhimsy

Carrie Anne K'iinuwaas Vanderhoop
@wampahaida
Youtube.com > UBC Learning Circle

Meredith Woolnough
meredithwoolnough.com.au
Society of Arts + Crafts: societyofcrafts.org
@meredithwoolnough

Organizations

American Astronomical Society: aas.org

American Craft Council: craftcouncil.org

Association of Forest and Nature Therapy Guides and
    Programs: natureandforesttherapy.org

British Crafts Council: craftscouncil.org.uk

Earthx, Inc.: earthx.org

Fiber Art Network: fiberartnow.net

Forest School Association: forestschoolassociation.org

Huckleberrywoman.com

International Astronomical Union: iau.org

International Dark Sky Association (IDA): darksky.org

Kaffe Fassett: KaffeFassett.com

Llano Earth Art Fest: llanoearthartfest.org

National Park Service (NPS): NPS.gov

Planet Earth: planetearth.com

Sculpture Nature: sculpturenature.com

Society of Crafts: societyofcrafts.org

Wild Wonder Nature Journaling Conference: johnmuir-
    laws.com/wildwonder

Hashtags

These hashtags led me through countless layers of
inspiration. I am adding them here in hopes that they
will spark your journey too.

#earthart

#environmentalart

#landart

#natureart

#naturefix

#natureinspired

#naturelover

#naturetherapy

#rewilding

#schiffercraft

#wildcrafting

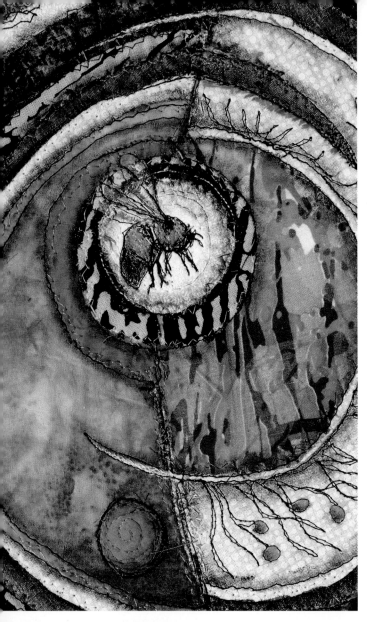

Books

Alger James. *At Home in the Woodlands: A Writer's Reflections on Nature*. CreateSpace, 2017.

Anderson, Lorraine. *Sisters of the Earth: Women's Prose and Poetry about Nature*. New York: Vintage Books, 2003.

Brandeis, Susan. *The Intentional Thread: A Guide to Drawing, Gesture, and Color in Stitch*. Atglen, PA: Schiffer, 2019.

Brown, Andrew. *Art and Ecology Now*. London: Thames & Hudson, 2014.

Cameron, Julia, and Eliza Foss. *The Listening Path: The Creative Art of Attention (a 6-Week Artist's Way Program)*. Audiobook. New York: St. Martin's Essentials, 2021.

Carruthers, Amelia, comp. and ed. *Writers on . . . Nature*. Redditch, UK: Read, 2014.

Earl, Sylvia PhD, and Bill McKibben, *The World Is Blue: How Our Fate and the Ocean's Are One*, National Geographic, 2009.

Elkins, James. *How to Use Your Eyes*. New York: Routledge, 2000.

Falick, Melanie. *Making a Life: Working by Hand and Discovering the Life You Are Meant to Live*. New York: Artisan, 2019.

Fox, Alice. *Natural Processes in Textile Art: From Rust Dyeing to Found Objects*. London: Batsford, 2015.

Franck, Frederick. *The Zen of Seeing: Seeing/Drawing as Meditation*. New York: Vintage, 1973.

Gilbert, Elizabeth. *The Signature of All Things: A Novel*. New York: Riverhead Books, 2013.

Goldsworthy, Andy. *Ephemeral Works*. New York: Harry N. Abrams, 2015.

Hedley, Gwen. *Drawn to Stitch: Line, Drawing and Mark-Making in Textile Art*. London: Batsford, 2020.

Hemachandra, Ray, and Karey Patterson Bresenhan. *500 Art Quilts: An Inspiring Collection of Contemporary Work*. New York: Lark Books, 2010.

Ivens, Sarah. *Forest Therapy: Seasonal Ways to Embrace Nature for a Happier You*. New York: Da Capo Lifelong Books, 2018.

James, Rosie. *Stitch Draw: Design and Technique for Figurative Stitching*. London: Batsford, 2014.

Laws, John Muir. *The Laws Guide to Nature Drawing and Journaling*. Berkeley, CA: Heyday, 2016.

Leslie, Clare Walker, and Charles E. Roth. *Keeping a Nature Journal: Deepen Your Connection with the Natural World All around You*. North Adams, MA: Storey, 2021.

Li, Dr. Qing. *Forest Bathing: How Trees Can Help You Find Help and Happiness*. New York: Penguin Life, 2018.

Lonning, Kari. *The Art of Basketry*. Self-published, 2000.

Lonning, Kari. *Akebia, from Invasive Vine to Fine Craft*. Self-published, 2018.

Lonning, Kari. *Inspired by Color*. Self-published, 2016.

MacFarlane, Robert. *Landmarks (Landscapes)*. London: Penguin UK, 2016.

Neddo, Nick. *The Organic Artist: Make Your Own Paint, Paper, Pigments, Prints and More from Nature*. Beverly, MA: Quarry Books, 2015.

Neddo, Nick. *The Organic Artist for Kids: A DIY Guide to Making Your Own Eco-friendly Art Supplies from Nature*. Beverly, MA: Quarry Books, 2020.

Parrott, Helen. *Mark Making: Fresh Inspiration for Quilt and Fiber Artists*. Loveland, CO: Interweave, 2013.

Roy, Lorraine. Woven Woods: A Journey through the Forest Floor. lroyart.com, 2019.

Sala, Enric. *The Nature of Nature: Why We Need the Wild*. Washington, DC: National Geographic, 2020.

Salamony, Sandra, and Gina Brown. *1000 Artisan Textiles: Contemporary Fiber Art, Quilts, and Wearables*. Beverly, MA: Quarry Books, 2010.

Schoeser, Mary. *Silk*. New Haven, CT: Yale University Press, 2007.

Schoeser, Mary. *Textiles: The Art of Mankind*. London: Thames & Hudson, 2012.

Selhub, M. Eva, and Alan C. Logan. *Your Brain on Nature: The Science of Nature's Influence on Your Health, Happiness, and Vitality*. Toronto: HarperCollins, 2014.

Seward, Linda. *The Art Quilt Collection: Designs and Inspiration from around the World*. New York: Sixth & Spring Books, 2010.

Simard, Suzanne. *Finding the Mother Tree: Discovering the Wisdom of the Forest*. New York: Alfred A. Knopf, 2021.

Tellier-Loumagne, Francoise. *The Art of Embroidery: Inspirational Stitches, Textures, and Surfaces*. London: Thames & Hudson, 2007.

Tompkins, Peter, and Christopher Bird. *The Secret Life of Plants*. New York: Harper & Row, 1989.

Wheelwright, Nathaniel T., and Bernd Heinrich. *The Naturalist's Notebook: An Observation Guide and 5-Year Calendar-Journal for Tracking Changes in the Natural World around You*. North Adams, MA: Storey, 2017.

Wohlleben, Peter. *The Hidden Life of Trees: What They Feel, How They Communicate—Discoveries from a Secret World*. Berkeley, CA: Greystone Books, 2016.

Woolnough, Meredith. *Organic Embroidery*. Atglen, PA: Schiffer Books, 2018.